THE STADIUM

Images and Voices of the Original Yankee Stadium

Photographs by Jon Plasse

Images and Voices of the

Original Yankee Stadium

For my dad,

Herman Plasse

My dad and I, holding

wend our way through the streets teeming with thousands of fans approaching the Stadium.

"Give me the best

hands tightly,

two tickets you got!"

My Dad tells the grizzled, cigar-smoking ticket seller.

We enter the Stadium, cross through the shadows, stopping briefly to purchase a scorecard and pencil with "New York Yankees" stenciled in gold.

Up the escalators and through tunnels, we climb higher and higher until we exit the last passageway, walk into the blinding sunlight, and then stop for a moment and stare:

The wide expanse of dazzling green grass.
The silky smooth brown infield dirt.
The undisturbed chalk batter boxes crowding home plate.

The usher takes us higher still into the stands, then stops, flips down and brushes off our seats. We sit and listen:

"Beer heah . . . Soda heah . . . Peanuts, get your peanuts. . . ."

I lick the mustard off my fingers after finishing my hot dog. Then, over the booming loudspeakers:

"Batting third, and playing center field. . . ."

I feel butterflies in my stomach.

"And the rockets red glare. . . ."

I hold my Yankee hat over my heart, shifting my feet impatiently.

And finally, the first batter slowly but deliberately waves his bat back and forth. The pitcher stares at home plate for a sign. The umpire crouches flat up against the catcher.

And now me and my dad, and thousands of other kids and their dads, are clapping, yelling, and screaming, waiting expectantly for that call first strike.

–**Jon Plasse**
Yankee Fan, Photographer

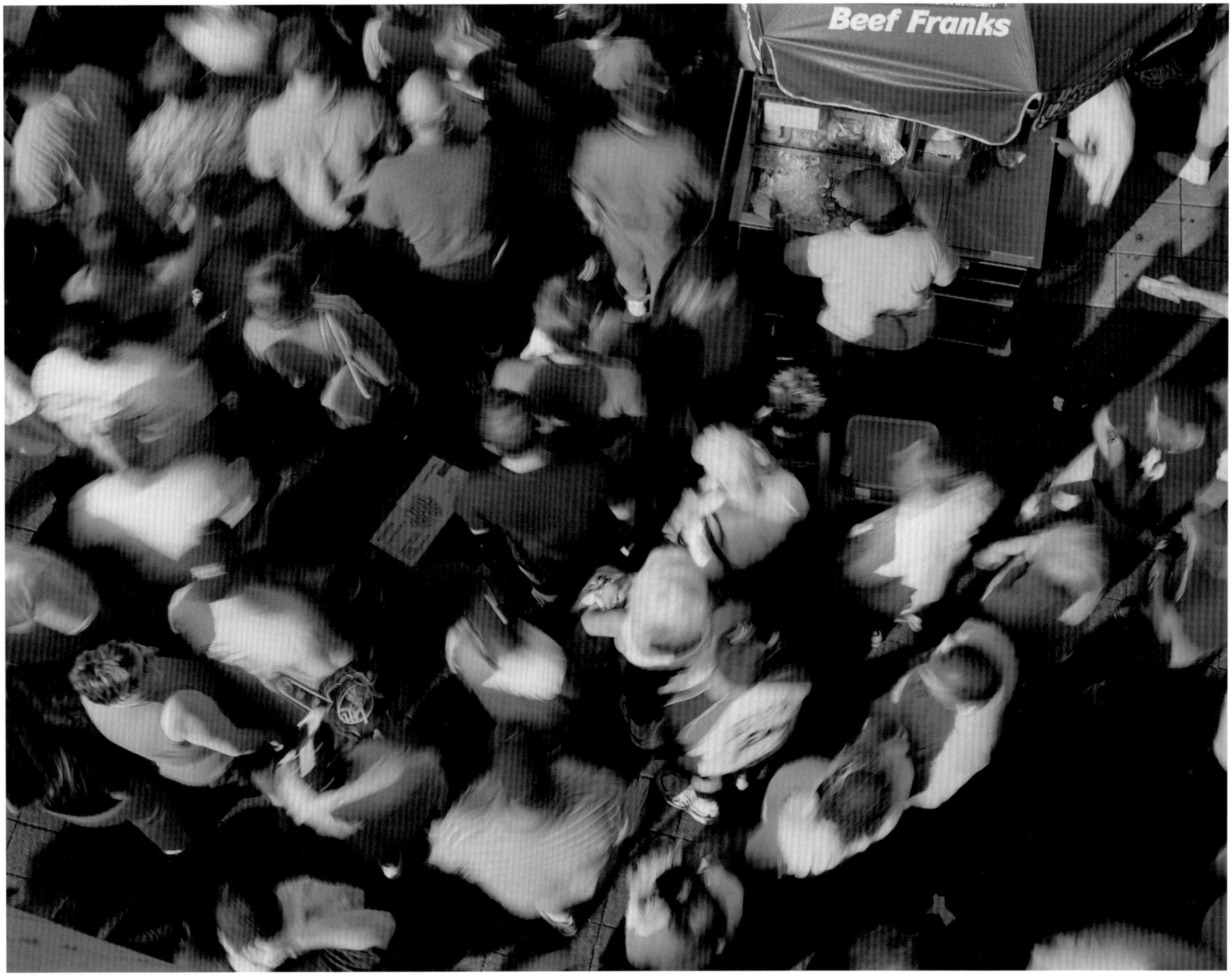
Beef Franks

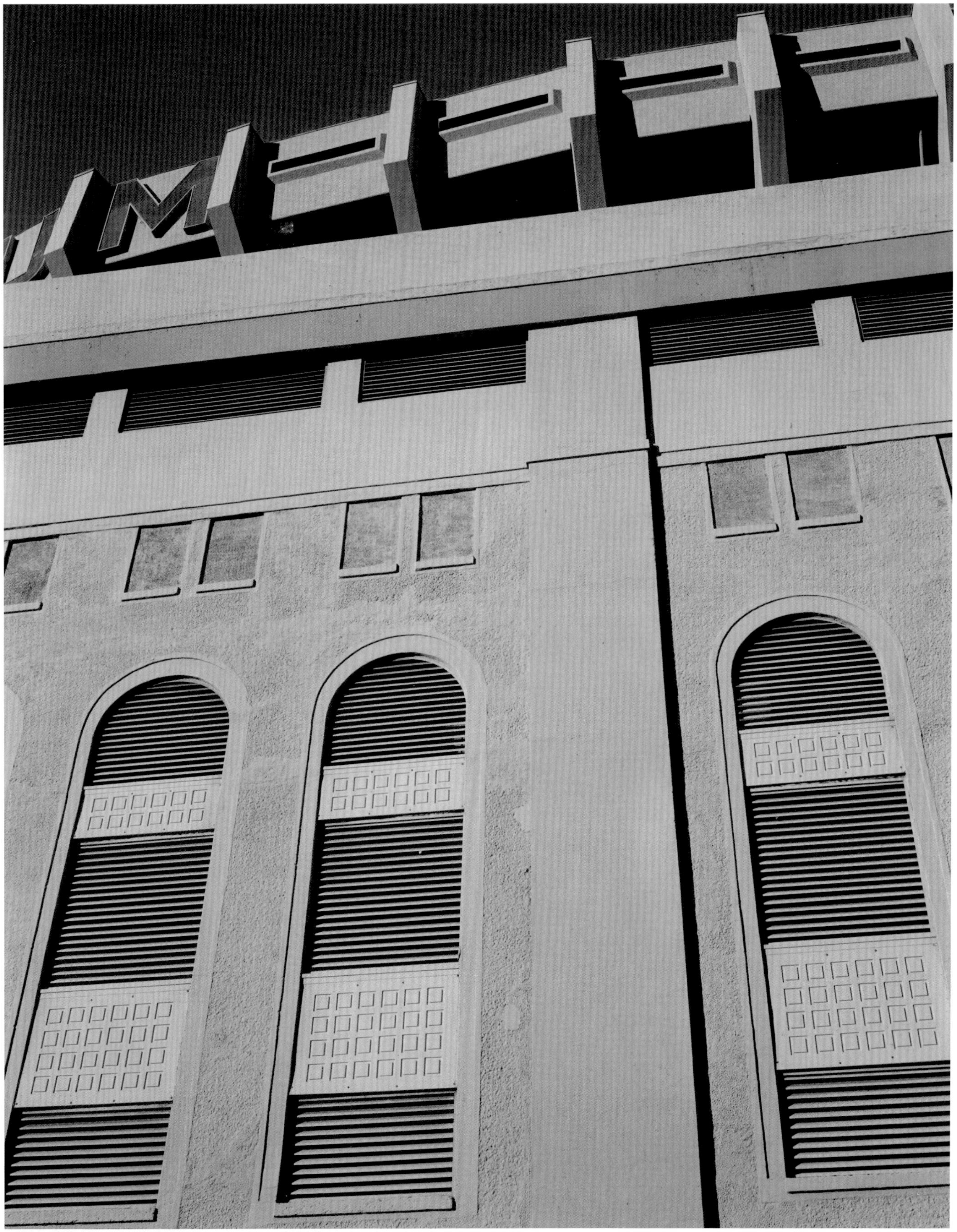

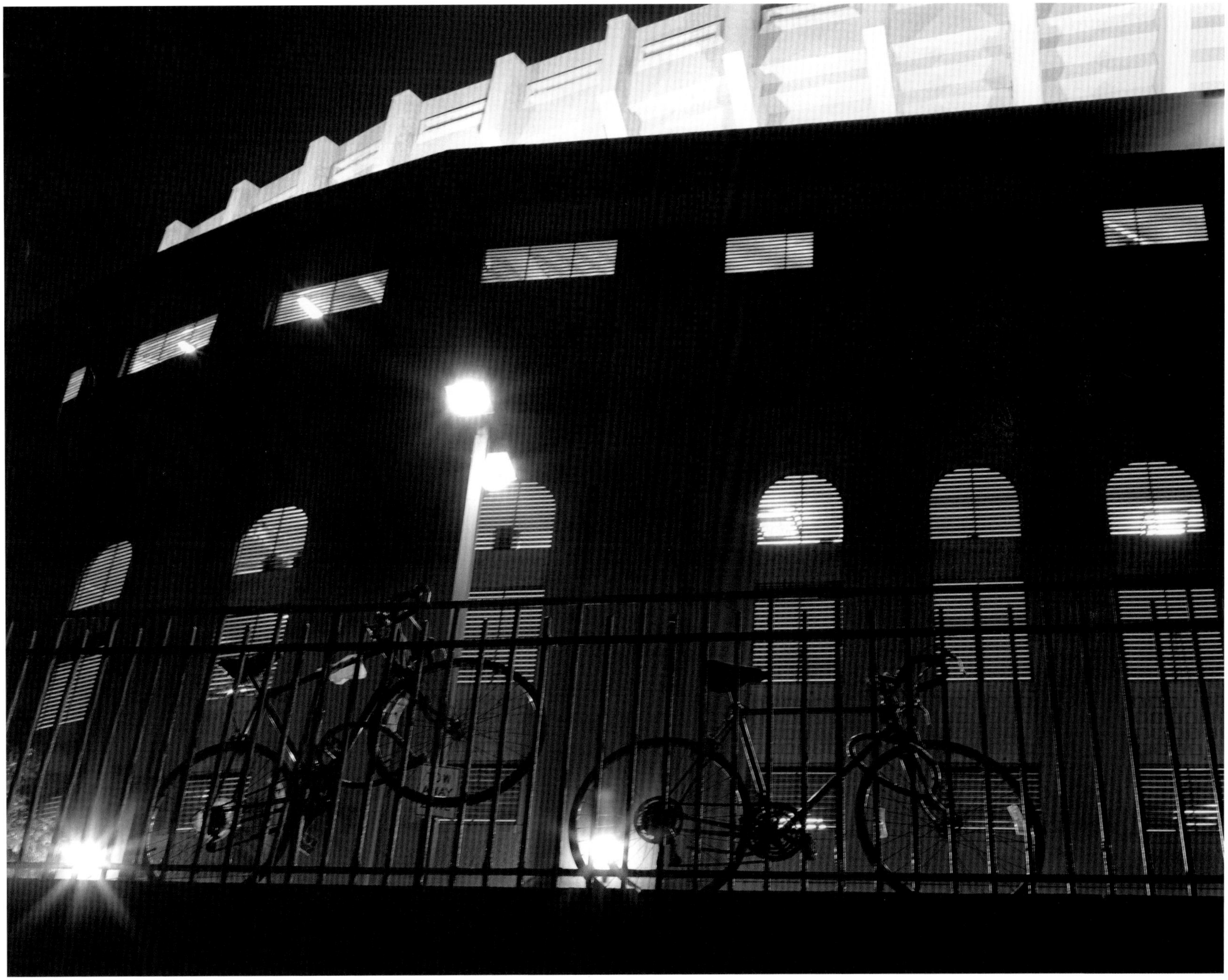

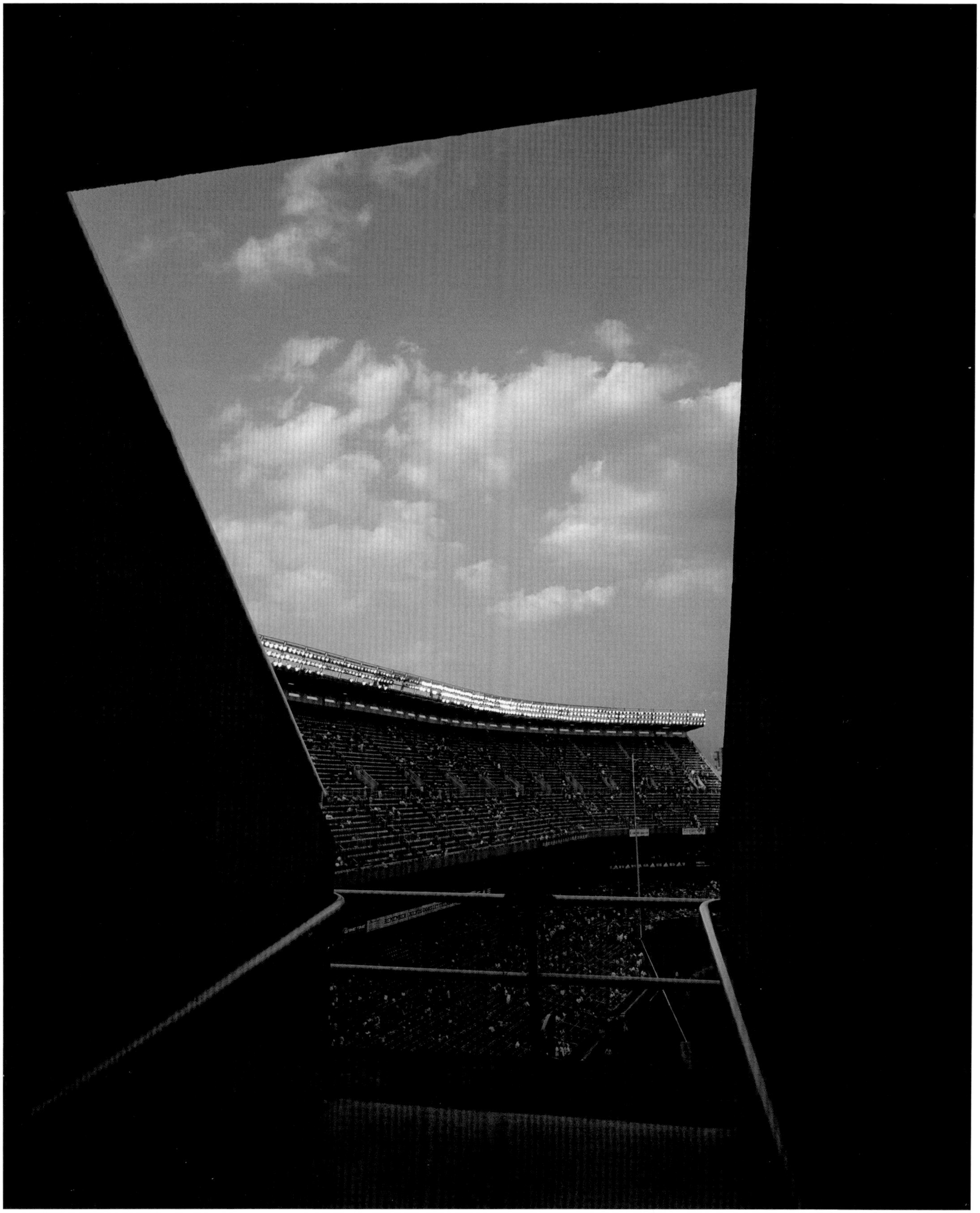

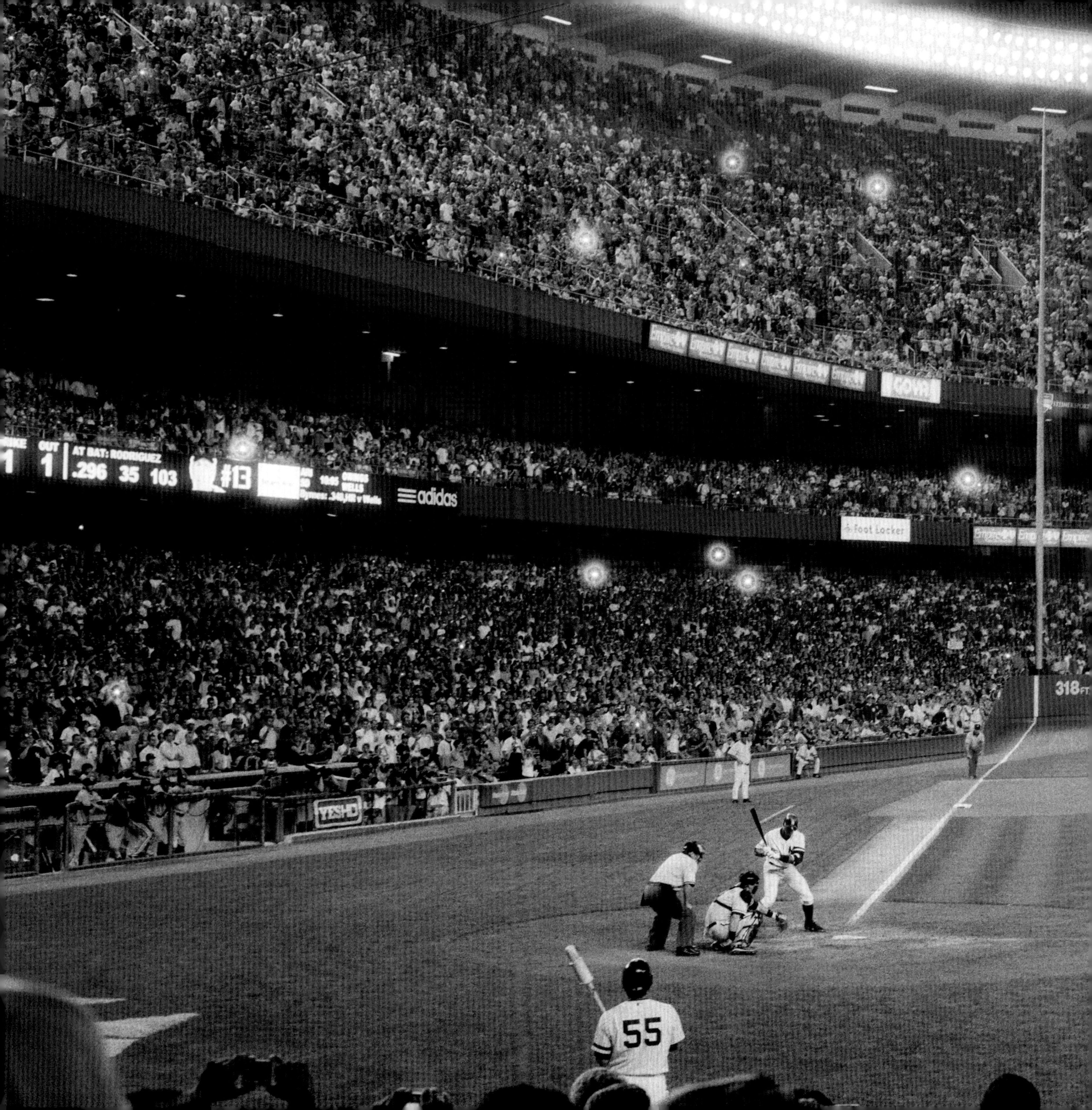
OUT
1
AT BAT: RODRIGUEZ
.296 35 103
#13
adidas
Foot Locker
318FT
YESHD
55

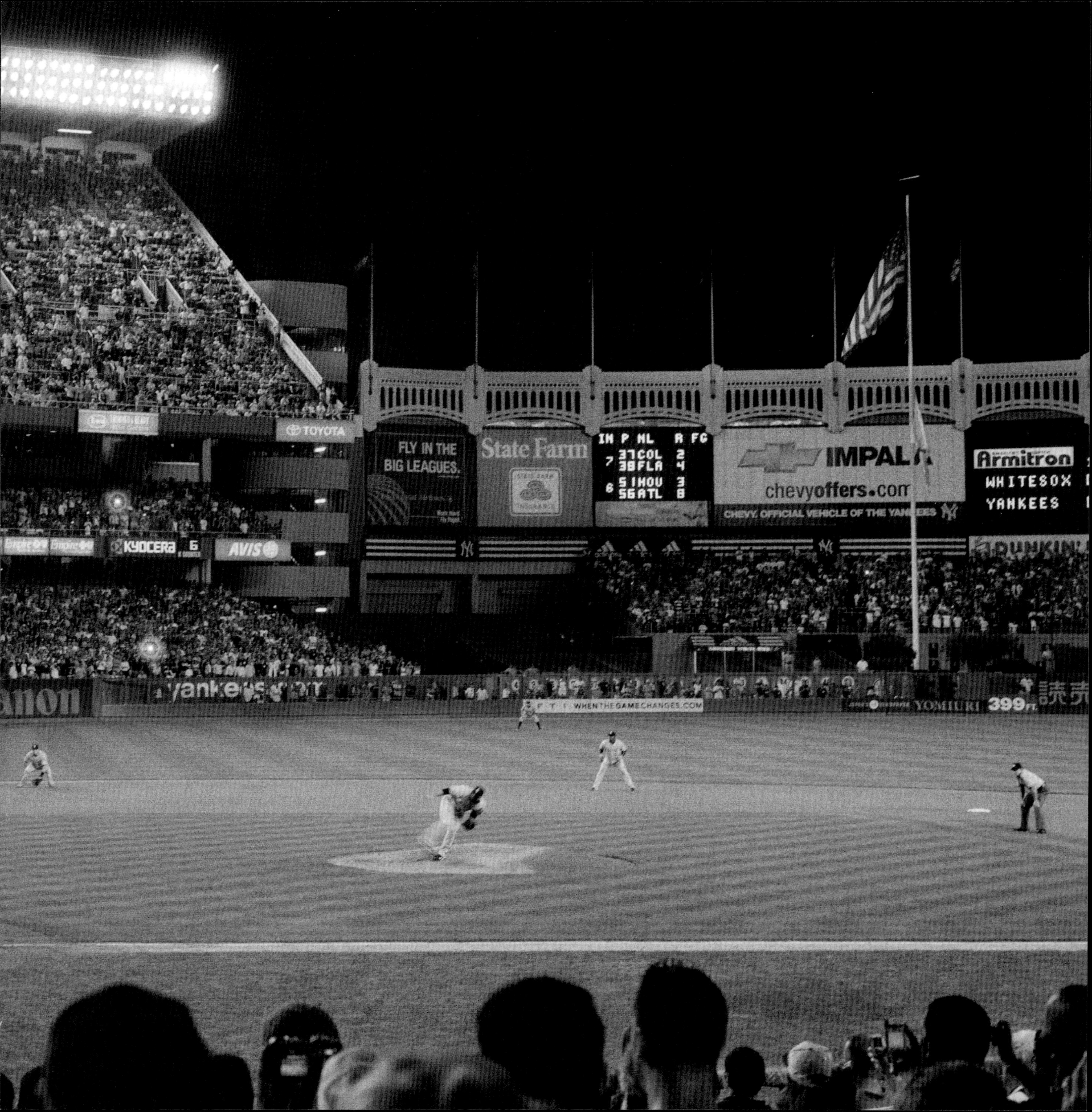
TOYOTA
FLY IN THE
BIG LEAGUES.
State Farm
IN P NL R FG
7 37 COL 2
38 FLA 4
6 5 HOU 3
56 ATL 8
IMPALA
chevyoffers.com
CHEVY. OFFICIAL VEHICLE OF THE YANKEES
Armitron
WHITESOX
YANKEES
KYOCERA
AVIS
yankees.com
WHENTHEGAMECHANGES.COM
YOMIURI
399 FT.

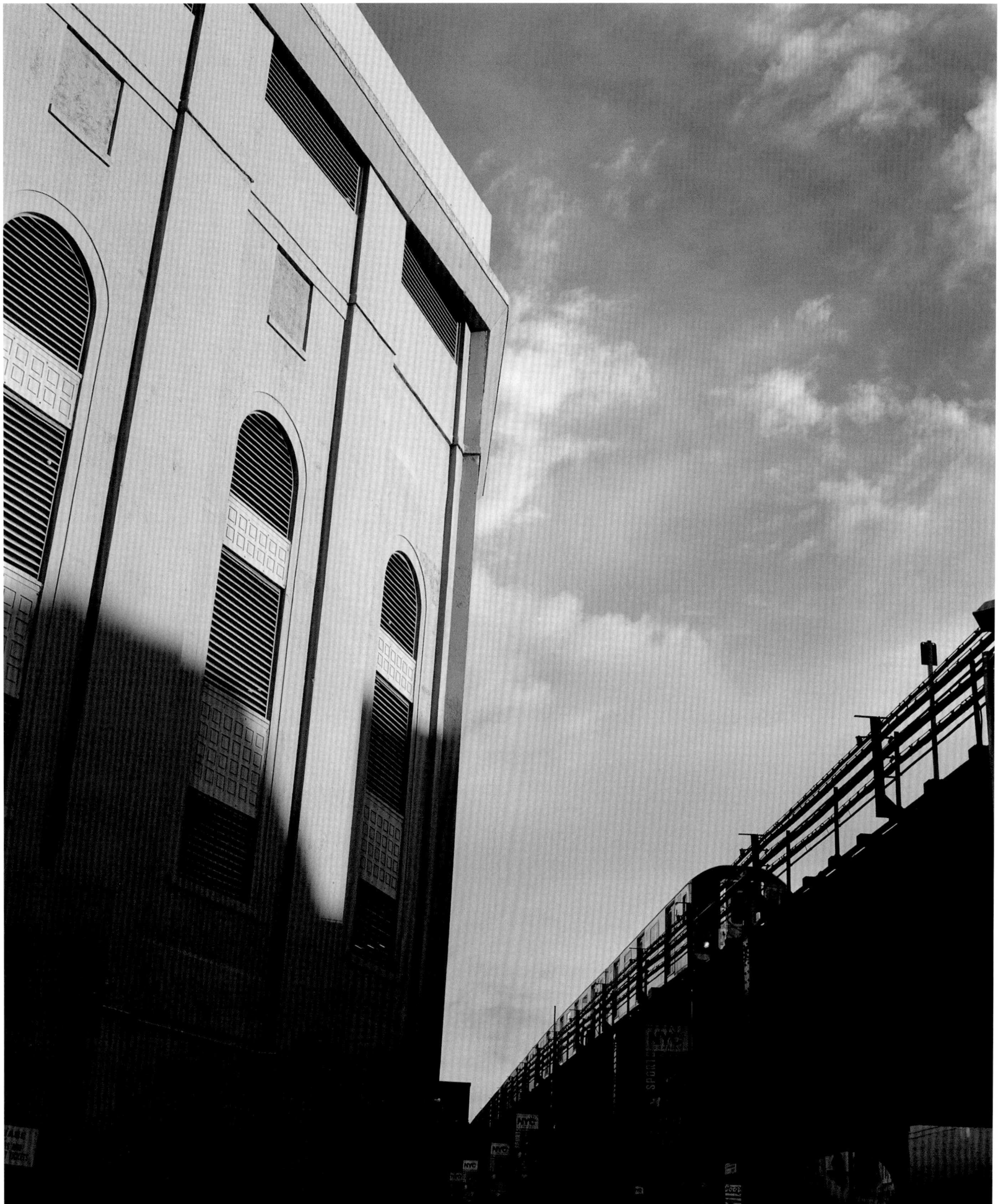

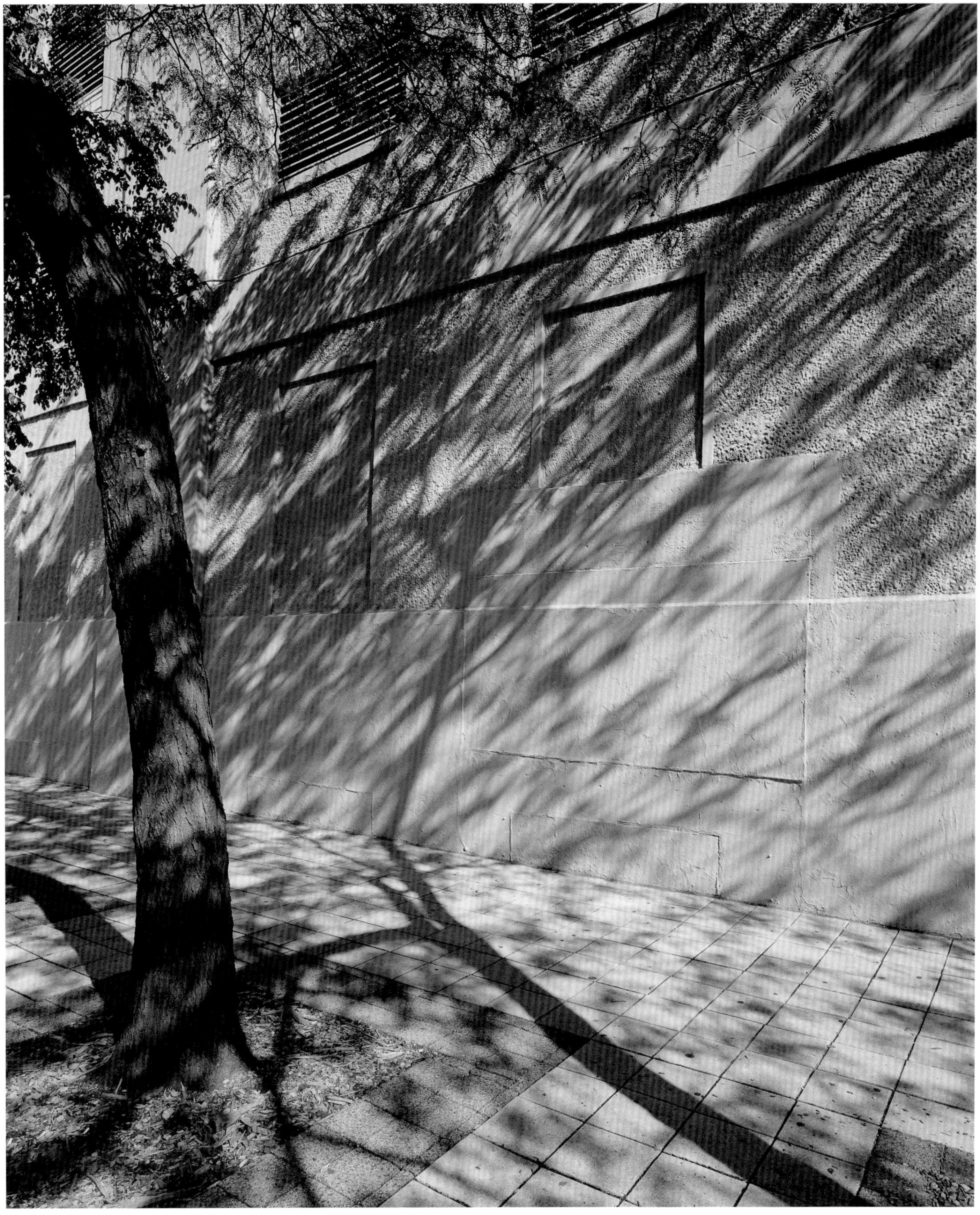

I first started

cotton candy, and pretzels at the Stadium when I was 14. I didn't graduate to hot dogs and beer until a couple years after. And they started me off slow by having me sell in the bleachers.

And sure, I was a big baseball fan, so I was always into the game while working.

Always trying to keep the game in the corner

selling ice cream,

what was going on with

of my eye.

But if I missed a play or two, I could still figure out what was happening by the crowd's reaction.

I mean as soon as there's a crack of the bat, if you see fans standing with their arms raised and their beer flies off–you know something good is happening.

Usually, the louder the roar, the bigger the play. And there was a certain roar where you knew the ball was hit really well and was going to be a home run –there'd be a build-up roar, it would get louder and louder and louder until the ball went out.

And then of course there were the boos . . . you know, nobody boos like a Yankee fan.

–Micheal Chaleff
Food Hawker

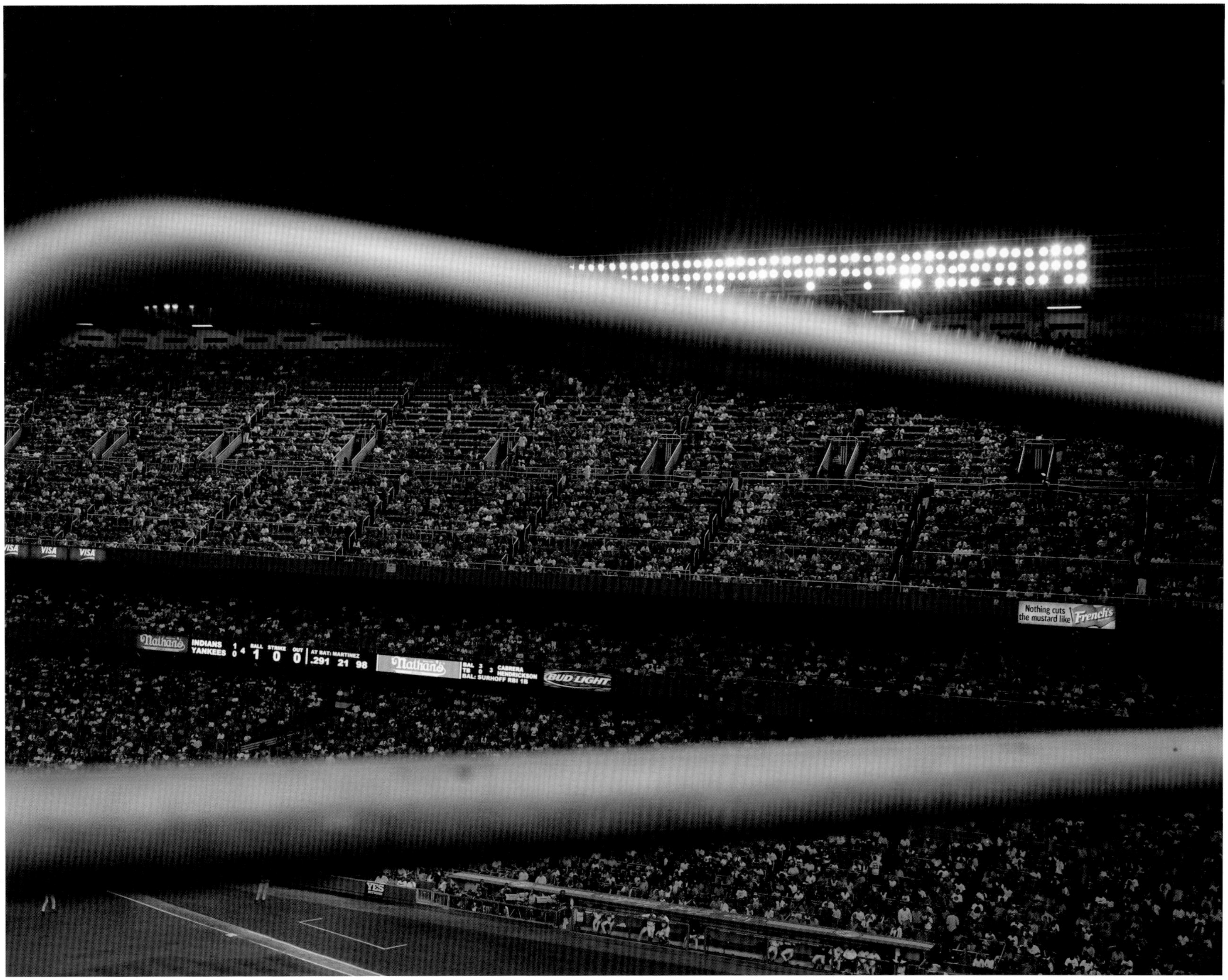

VISA VISA VISA
Nathan's
INDIANS 1 4
YANKEES 0
BALL 1 STRIKE 0 OUT 0
AT BAT: MARTINEZ
.291 21 98
Nathan's
BAL 3 3 CABRERA
TB 0 HENDRICKSON
BAL: SURHOFF RBI 1B
BUD LIGHT
Nothing cuts the mustard like French's
YES

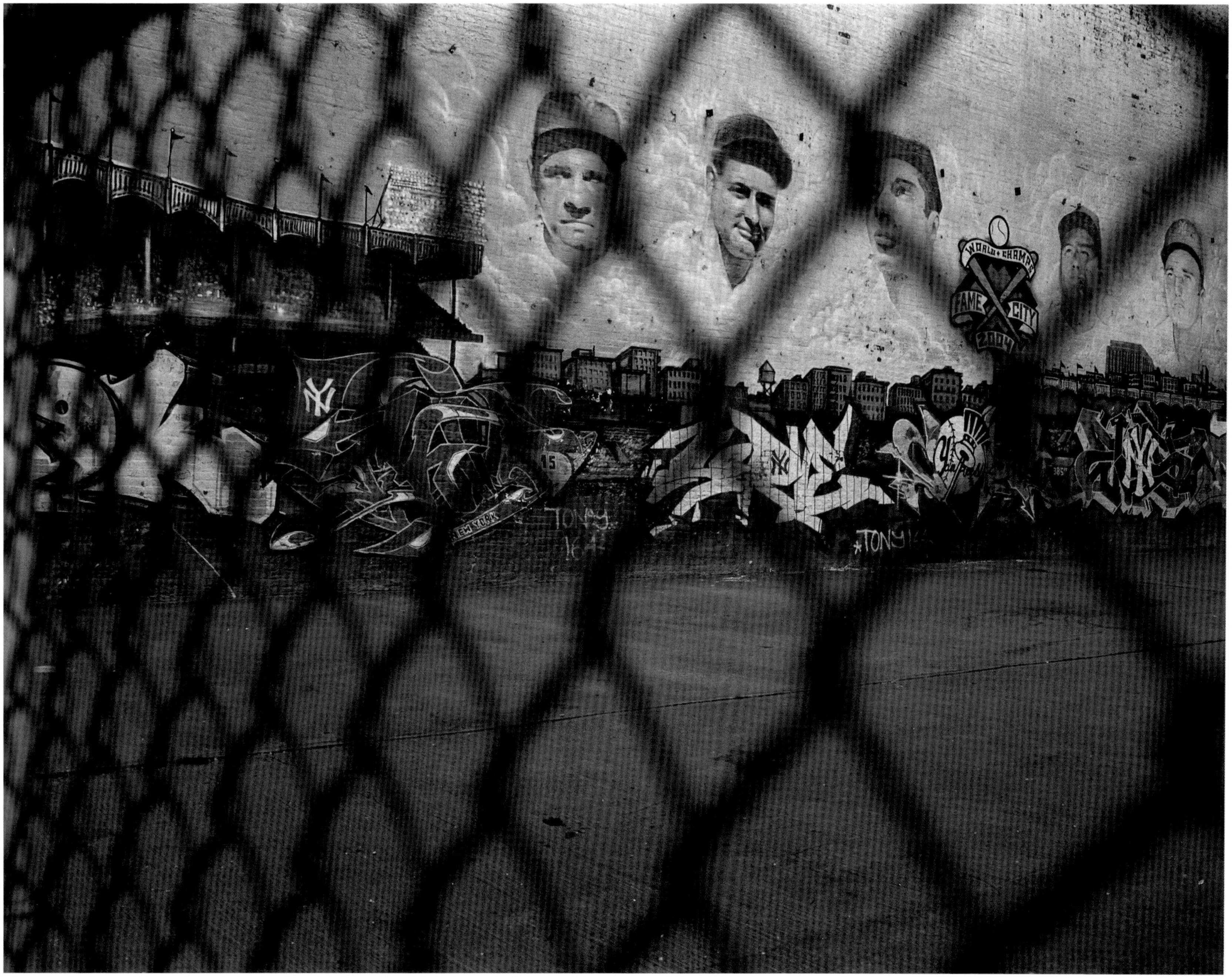
NY
FAME
CITY

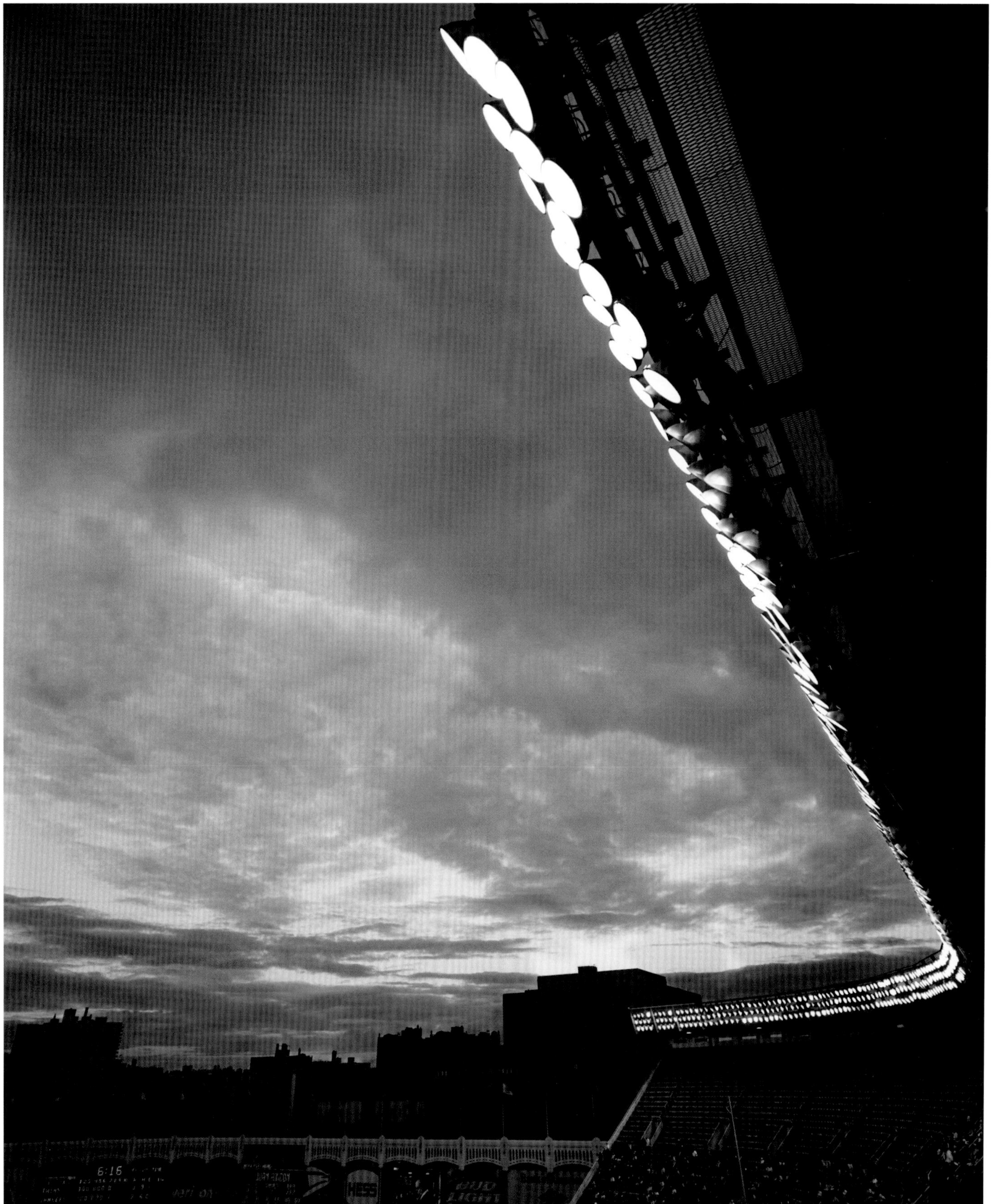
HESS

I still remember the first time

it was just awesome.

I left my dressing room, walked through the tunnel and Yankee dugout, and climbed up onto the field.

And there it was, the

a palace of baseball.

walked into the Stadium;

Stadium, gorgeous, just

It had those facades and everything, the stands filled with those noisy fans, the monuments out in center field.

And I guess I felt the ghost of Babe Ruth, or something.

I got a tear in my eye, my heart just skipped a beat.

I umpired for 18 years, would go to Fenway, which had a history, Cleveland—that big huge monster of a municipal stadium, or Comiskey Park in Chicago, and every other major league field. But there was absolutely nothing, *nothing like the experience of walking for that first time onto the field at the Stadium.* You ask any other umpire, coach, trainer, or player, and they'll tell you the same thing.

–Bill Valentine
American League Umpire

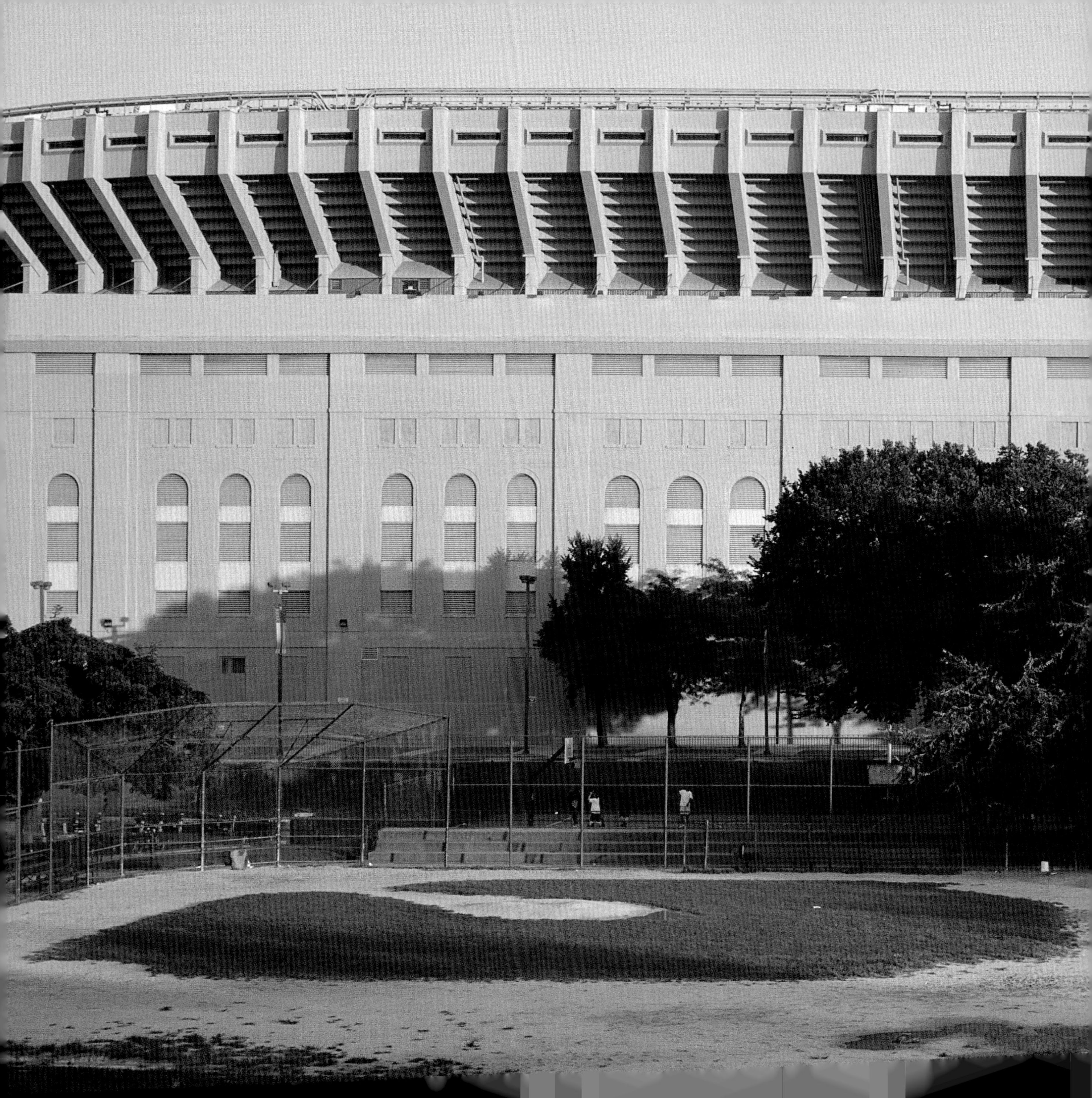

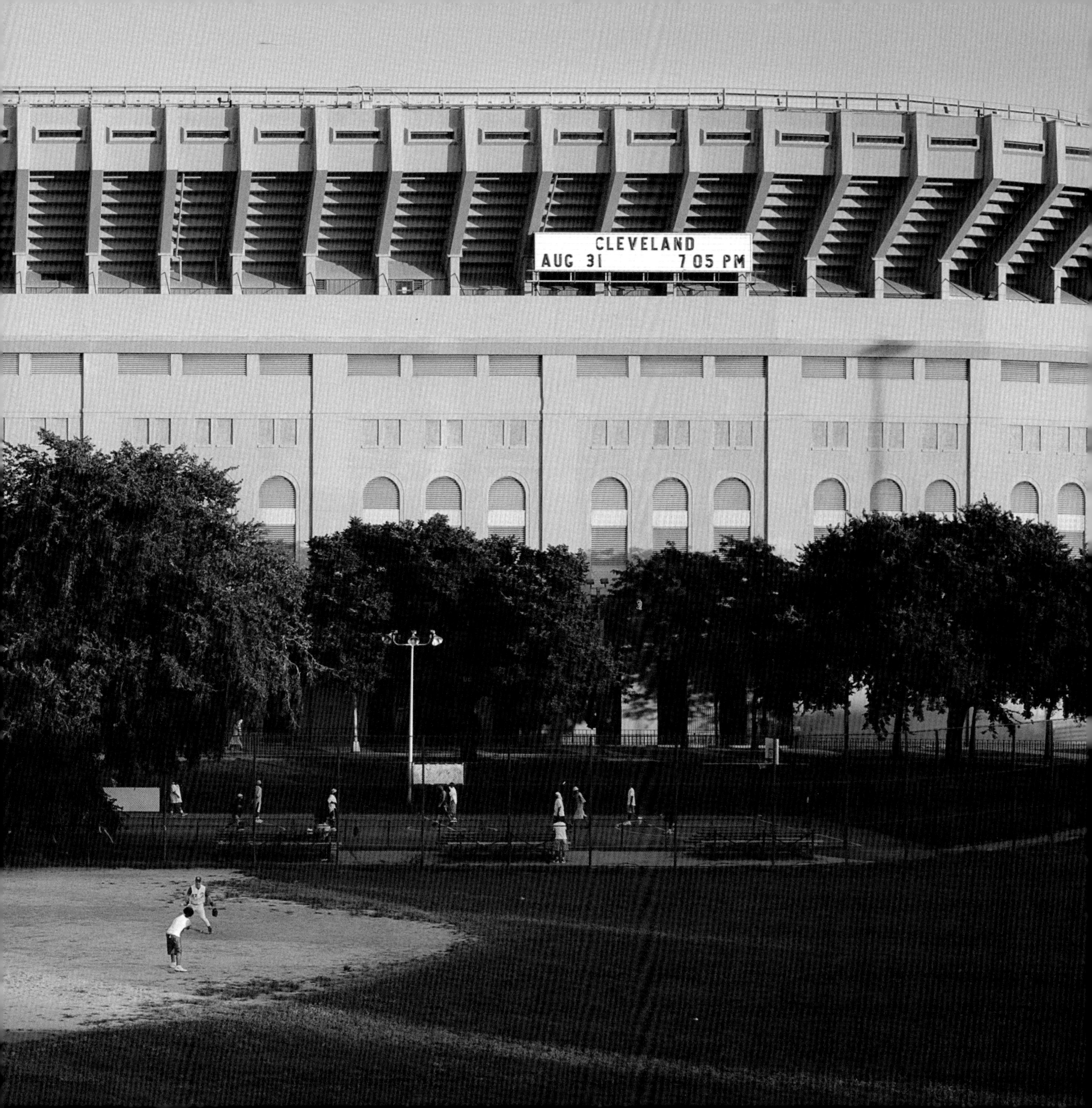
CLEVELAND
AUG 31 7 05 PM

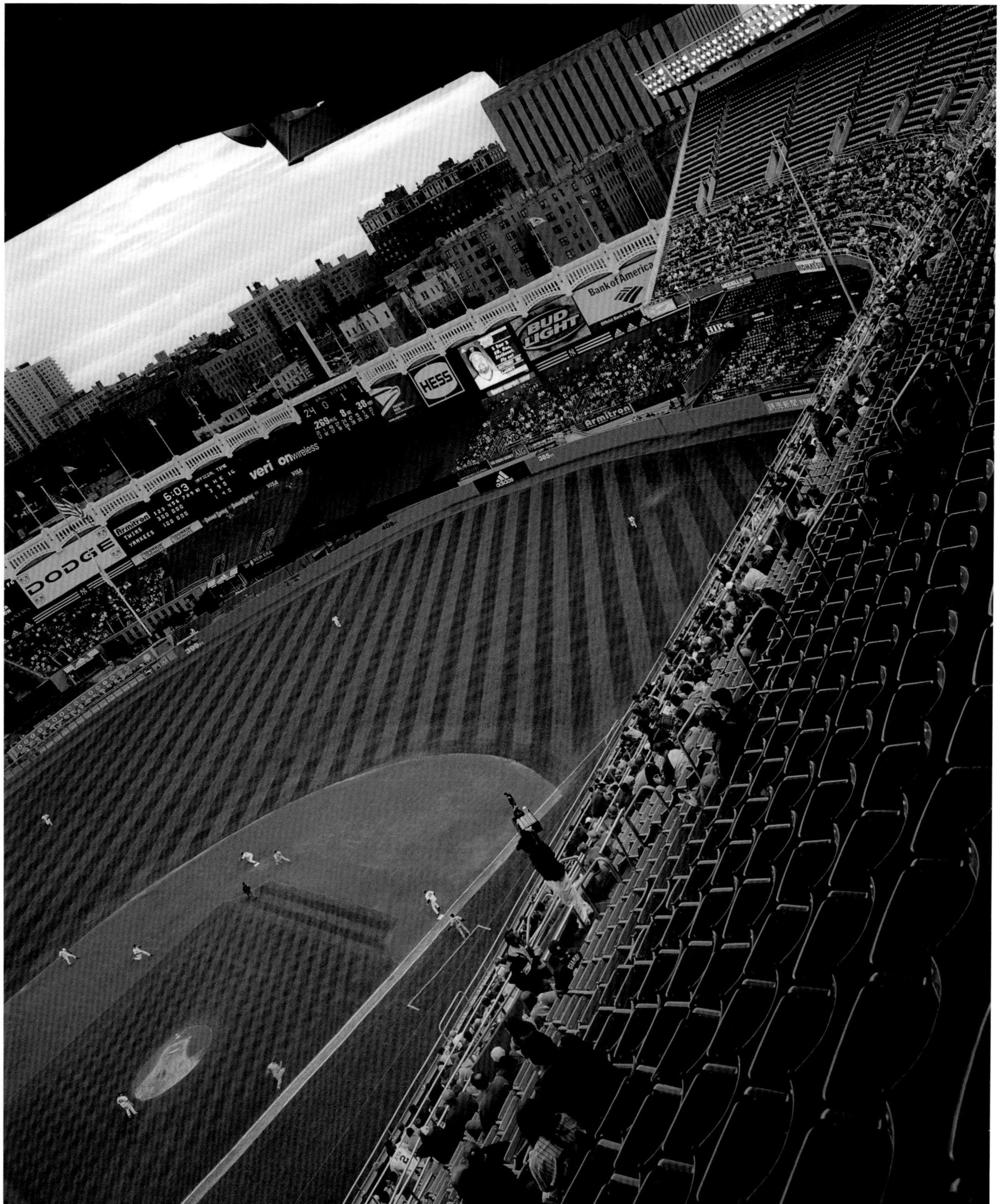
Bank of America
BUD LIGHT
HESS
DODGE
Armitron
6:03
TWINS
YANKEES

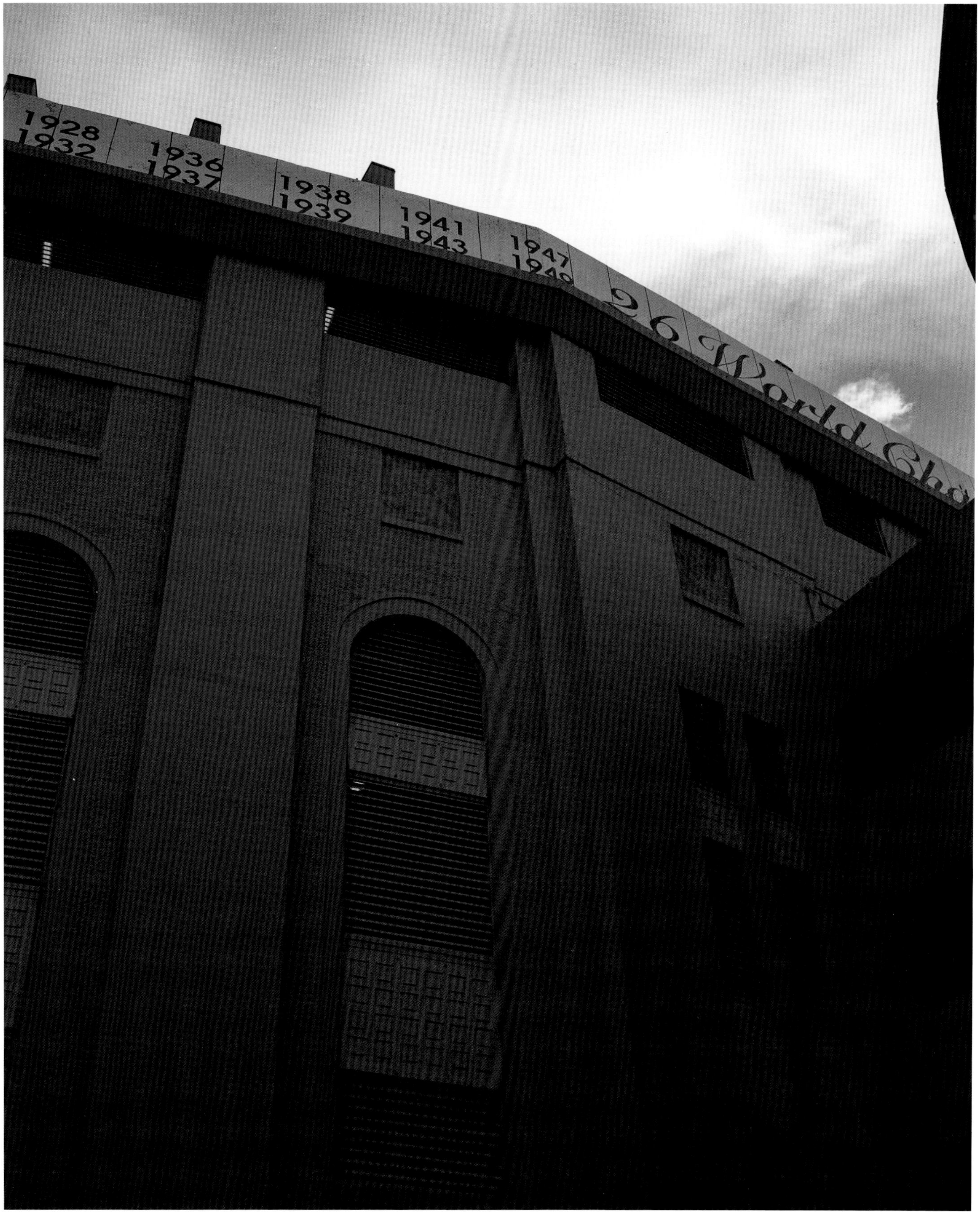
1928
1932
1936
1937
1938
1939
1941
1943
1947
26 World

Went to my first game ir

I liked the "old Stadium" a lot, before it was fixed up in '76. Back then, you could walk right onto the outfield after the game.

But you had to be careful: you could get a seat right behind one of those poles, blocking your view. But it wasn't so bad: you'd just wait a while for an empty seat, then move, and watch the game.

By 1990, I had retired, but I still wanted to do something.

I heard they were hiring would happen, but I got

43, when I was 9 years old.

ushers. I never thought it

the job.

So, I was a Yankee usher in '90 and '91. Usually worked the box seats. Fans would come in, parents and their kids, all smiles and excited. Some didn't have tickets to go down to the field, but I'd let them go anyway, let them get autographs, take pictures. Kids asking, "when's the game gonna start?" Bob Shepherd, the way he talked, that calm, he didn't rush it. Batters swinging, everyone, kids and adults, running for those foul balls.

It was a great place to see a game.

–Eddie DeJesus
Yankee Stadium Usher

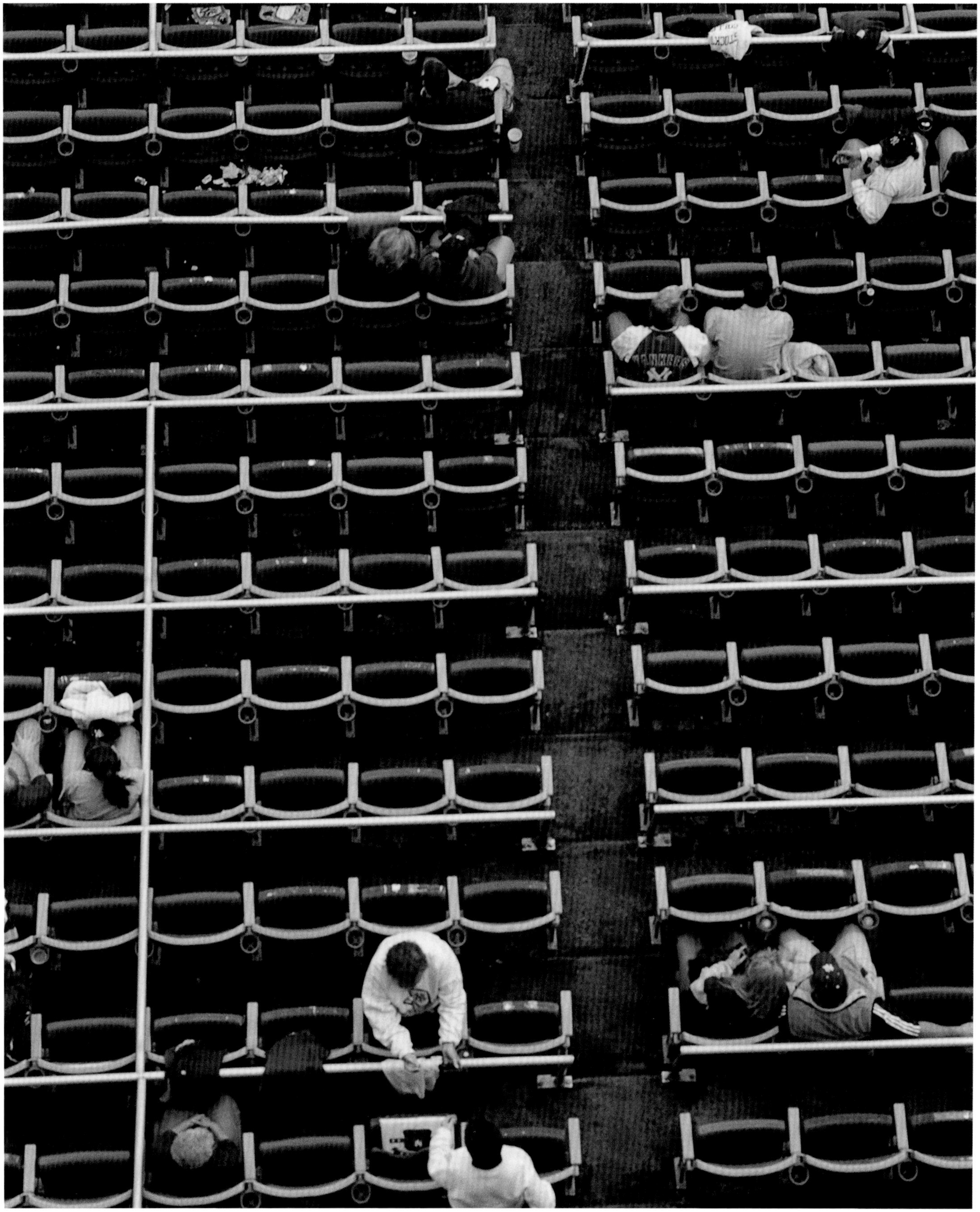

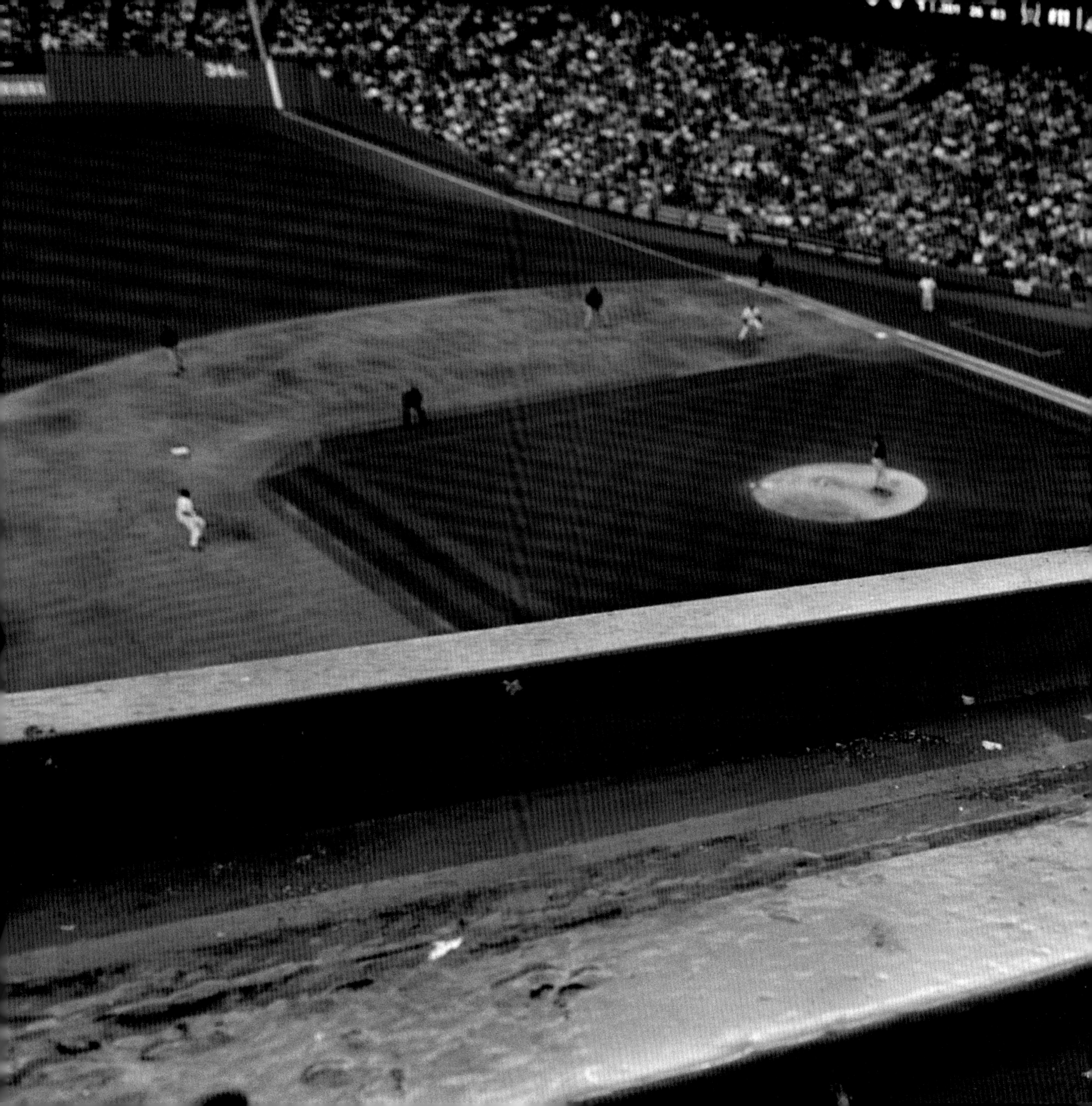

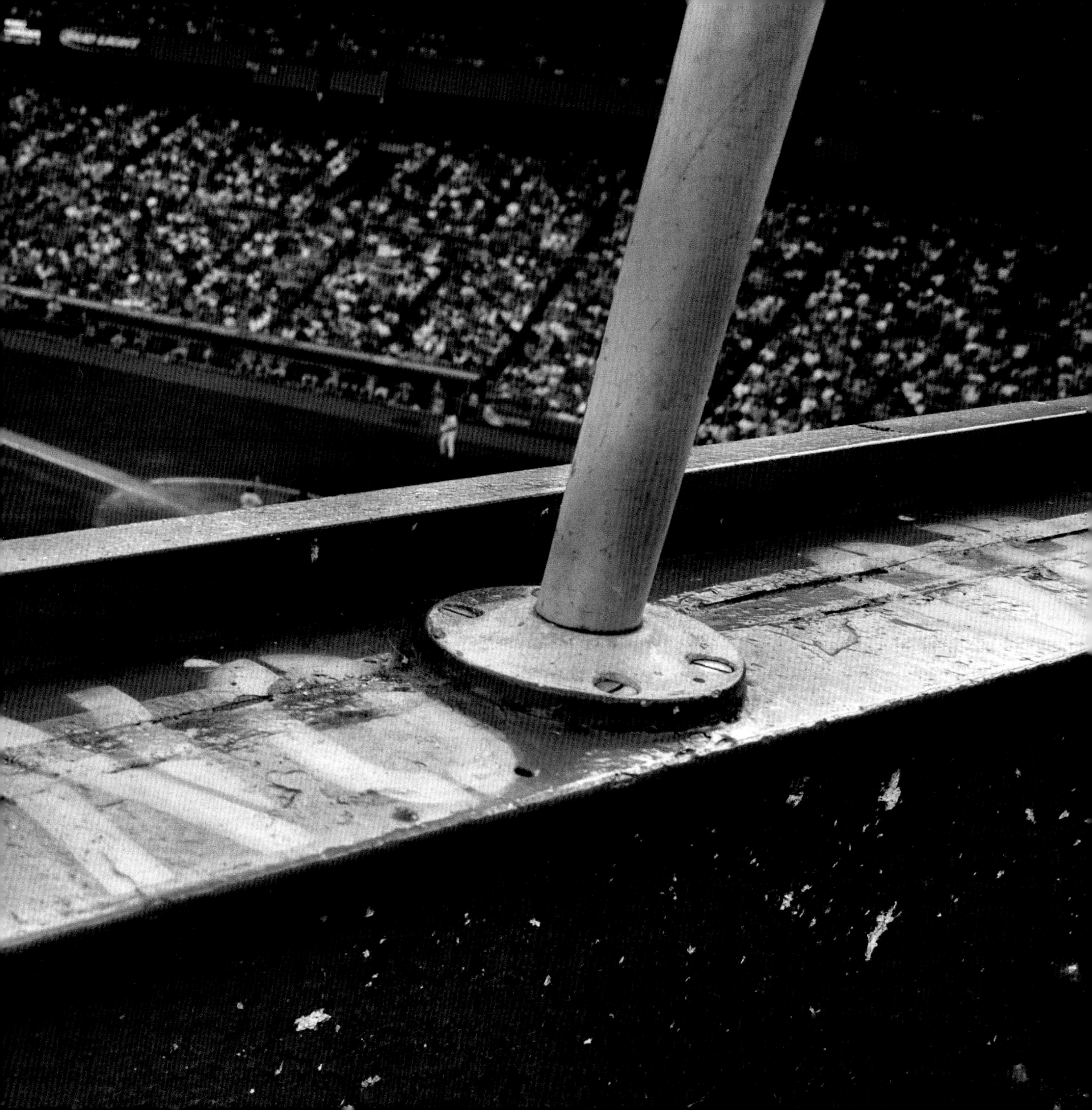

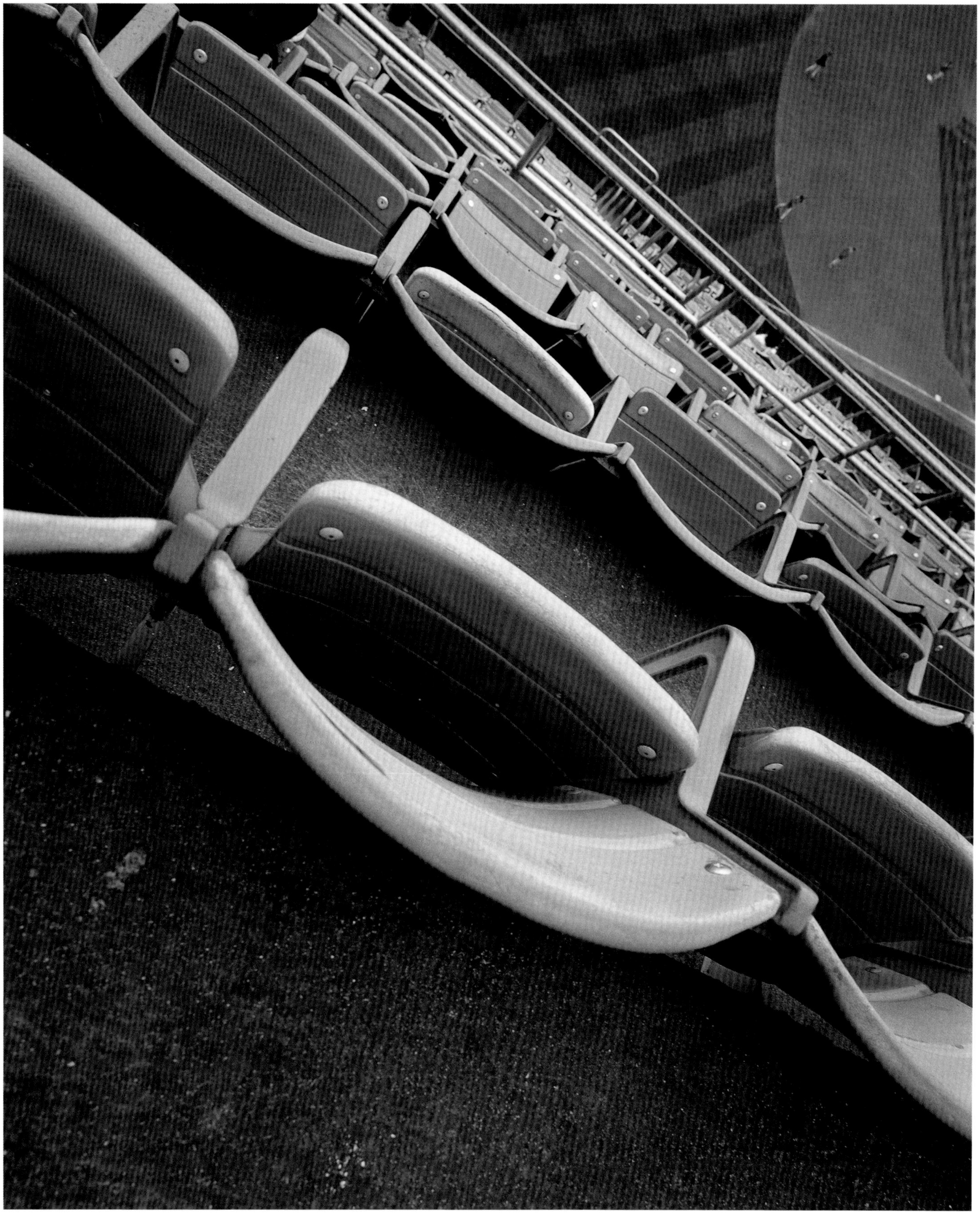

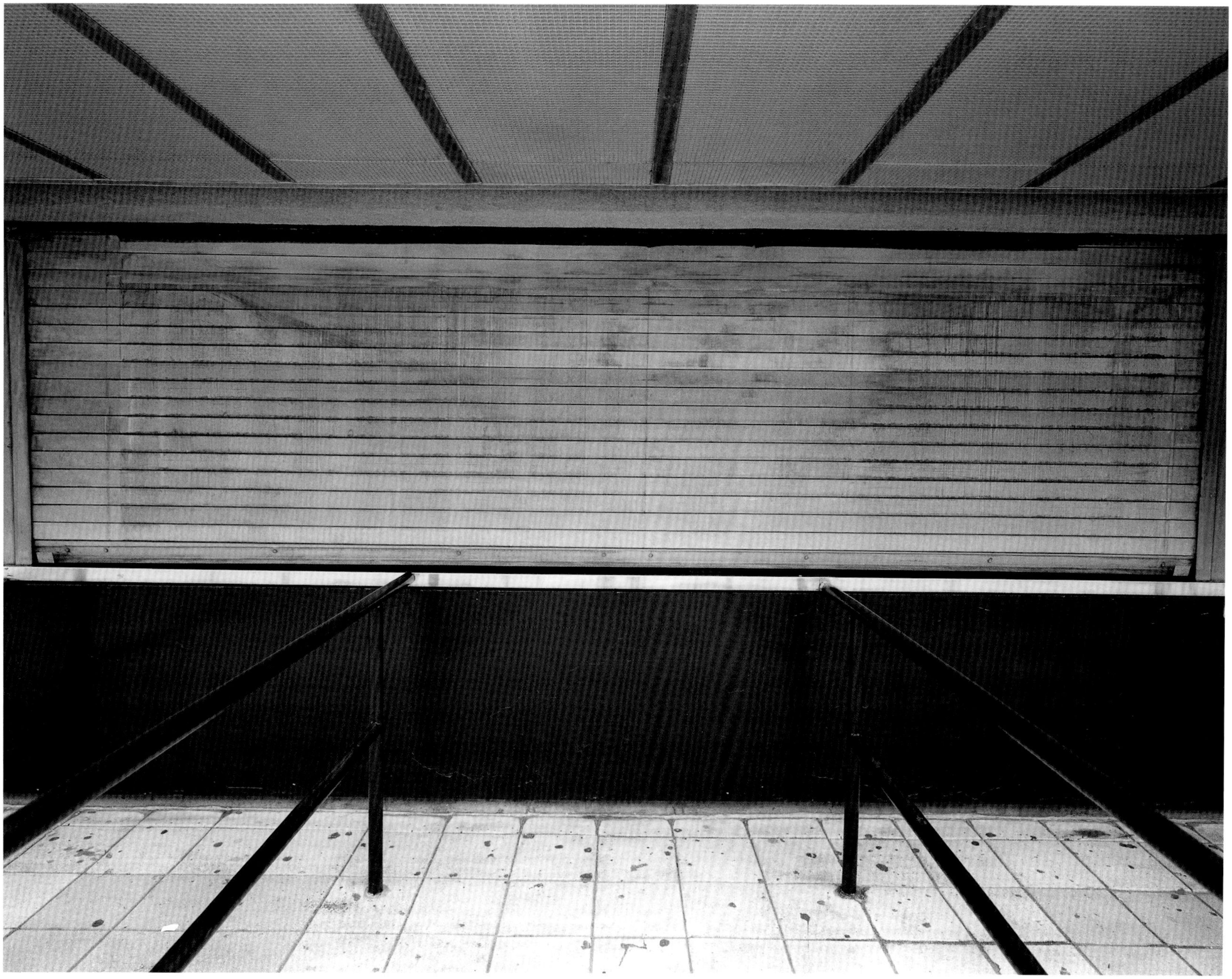

We ran a series of shops

filled with a wide variety of products: t-shirts, headwear, you name it, we had it. And the kids, they would come into our stores, their eyes running over the racks, their dads chasing after them. And they usually knew exactly what they wanted, would run up and grab it, and we'd have the scissors there to take the labels off right away.

Then they'd put on their new on their faces, and off they'd

behind home plate,

Yankee t-shirts, huge smiles go to watch the game.

And there were always certain numbered jerseys that were the most popular—number 2 on the v-necks, that was always the top one. Following that, I'd probably say number 13, and after that 42. Some years number 22.

And then there were the old timers: number 7, that was definitely the best.

–Matt Perachi
Yankee Stadium Merchandise Manager

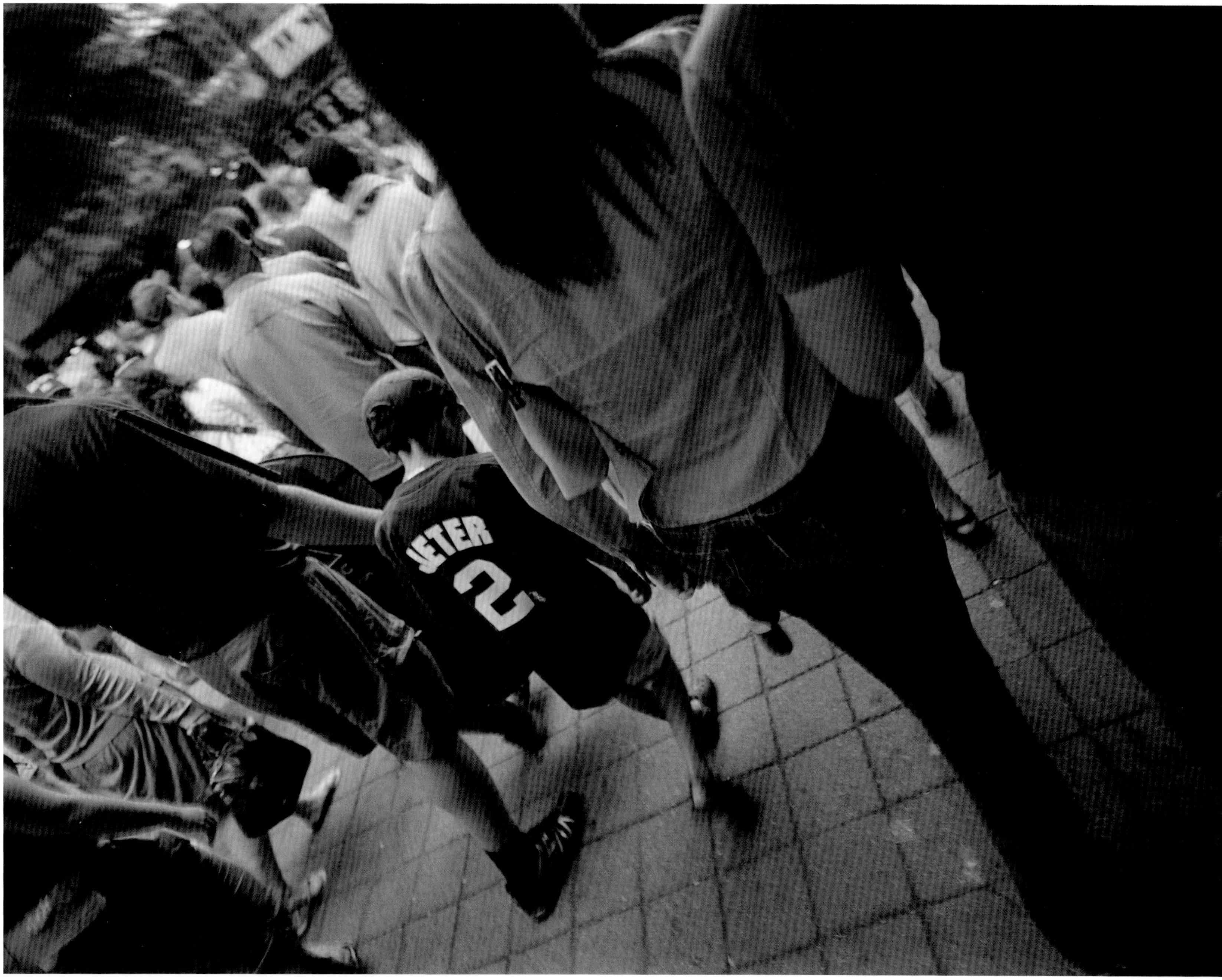
JETER
2

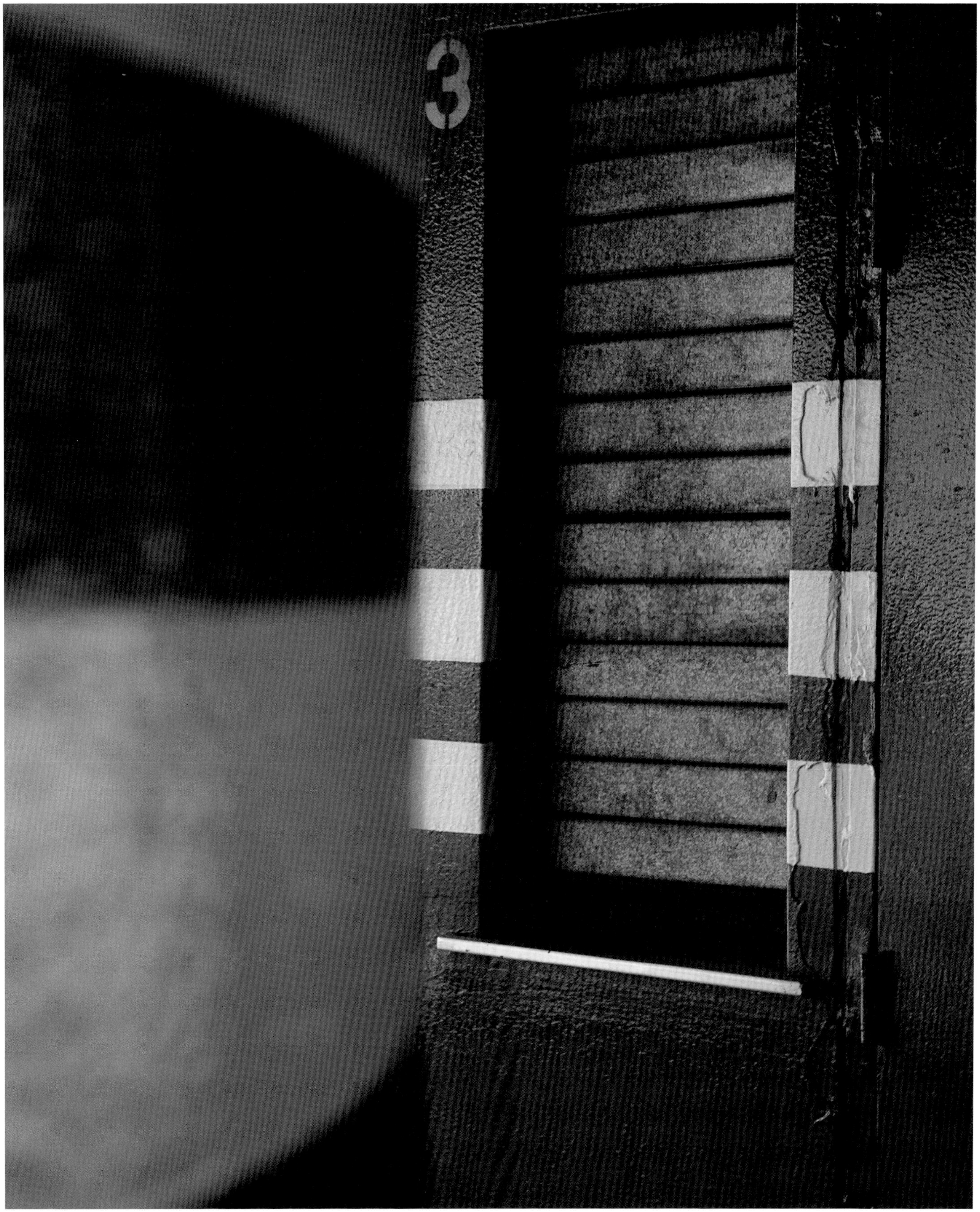
3

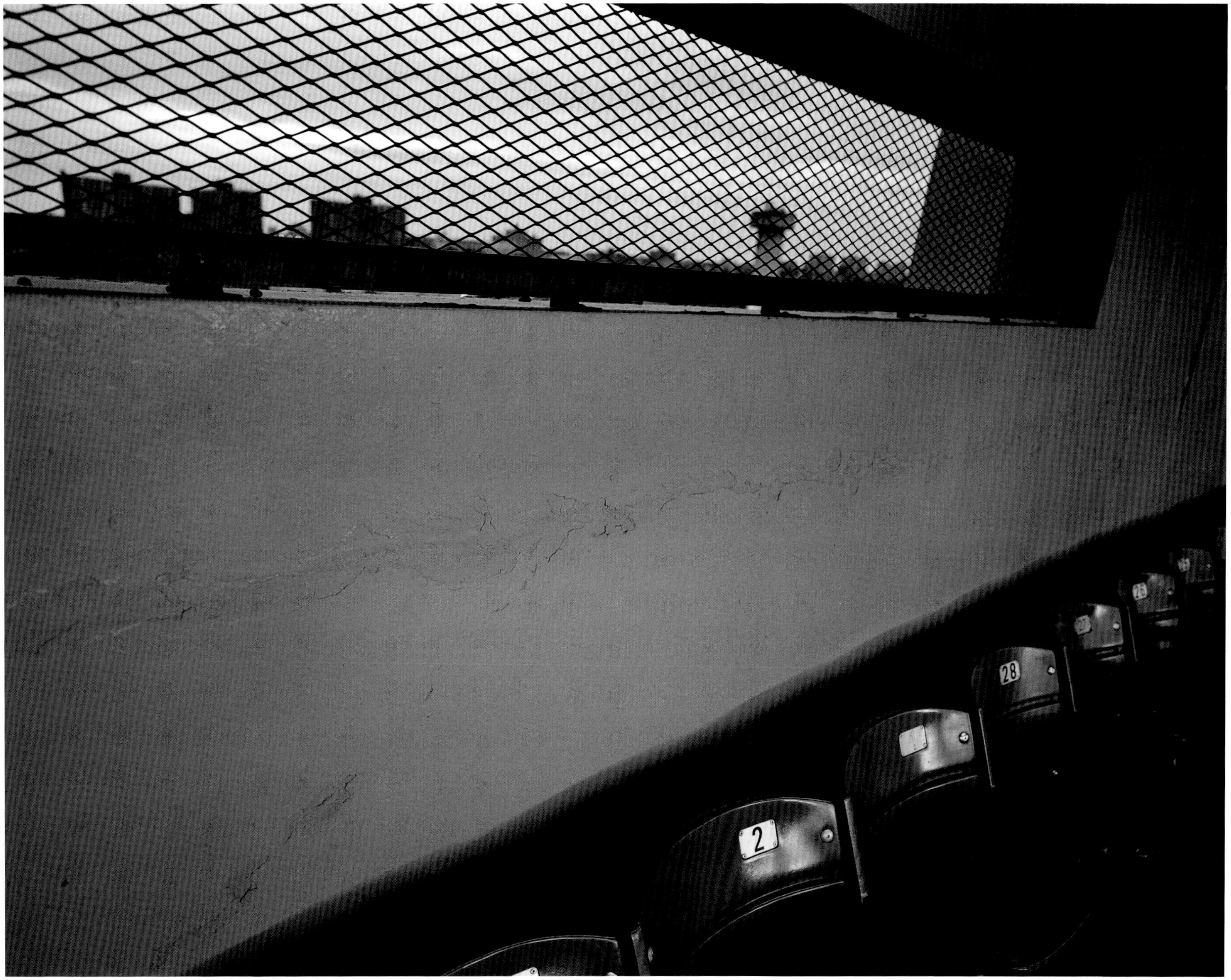
28
2

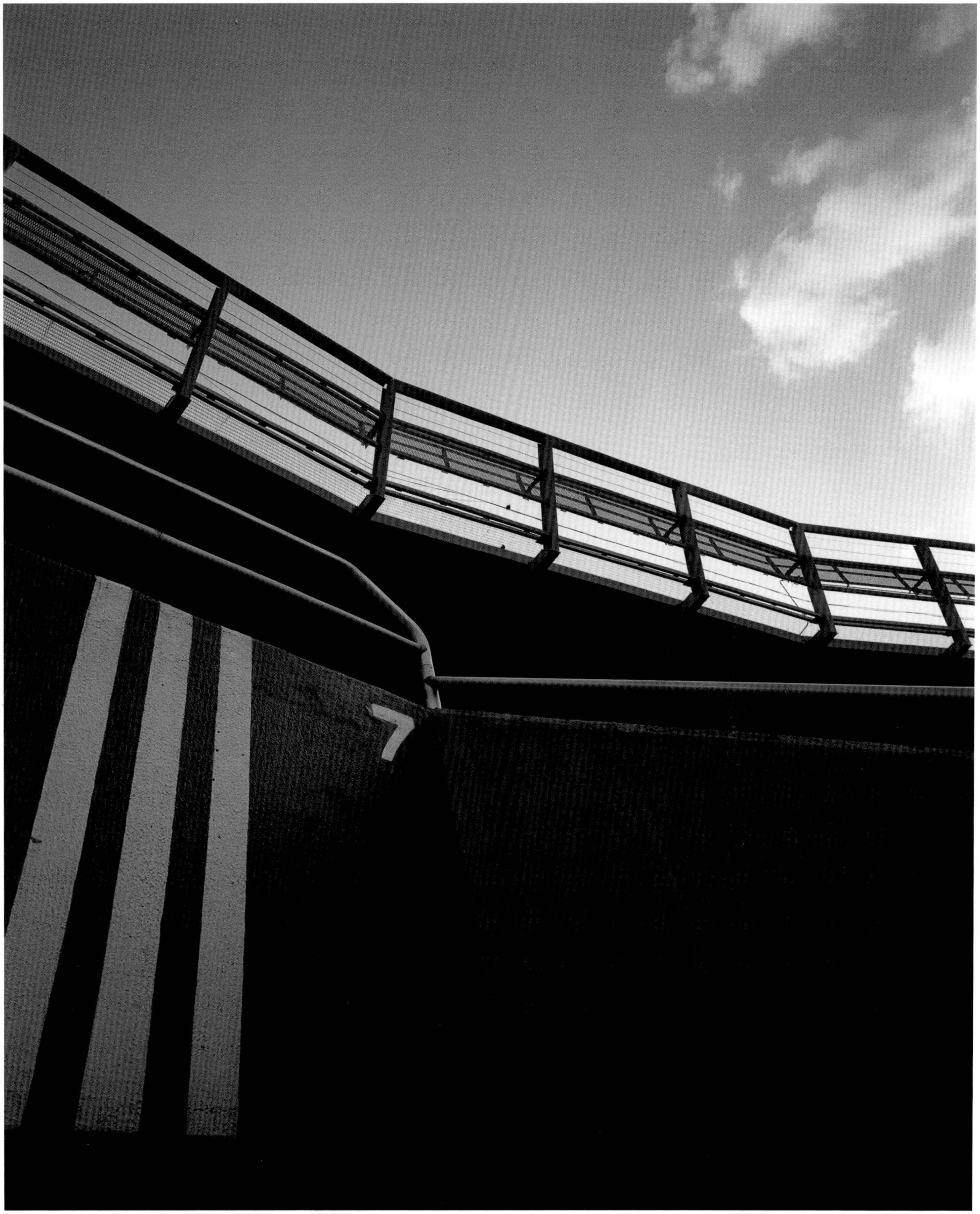
7

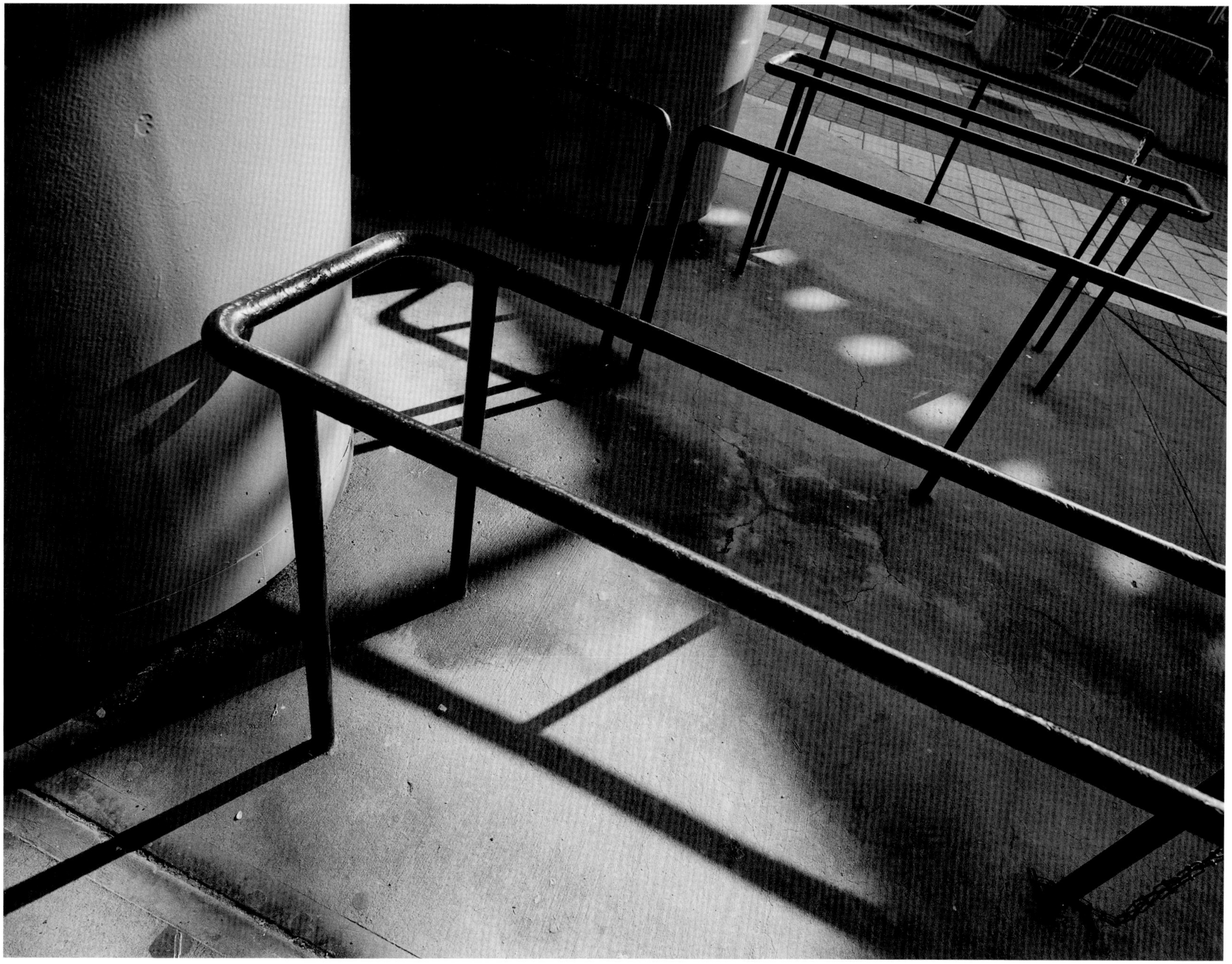

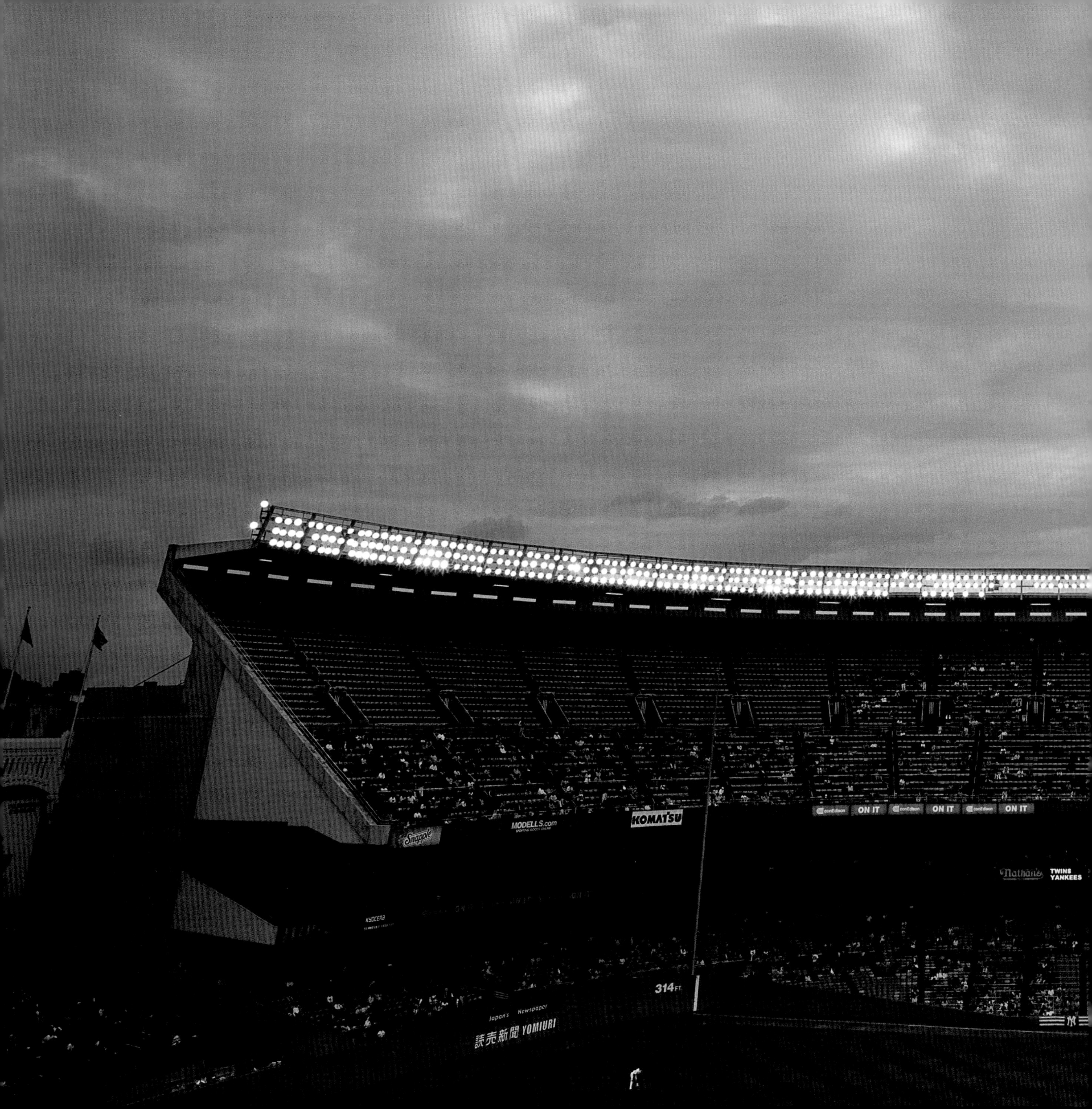
KOMATSU
ON IT
ON IT
ON IT
MODELLS.com
Snapple
Nathan's
TWINS
YANKEES
KYOCERA
314 FT.
Japan's Newspaper
読売新聞 YOMIURI

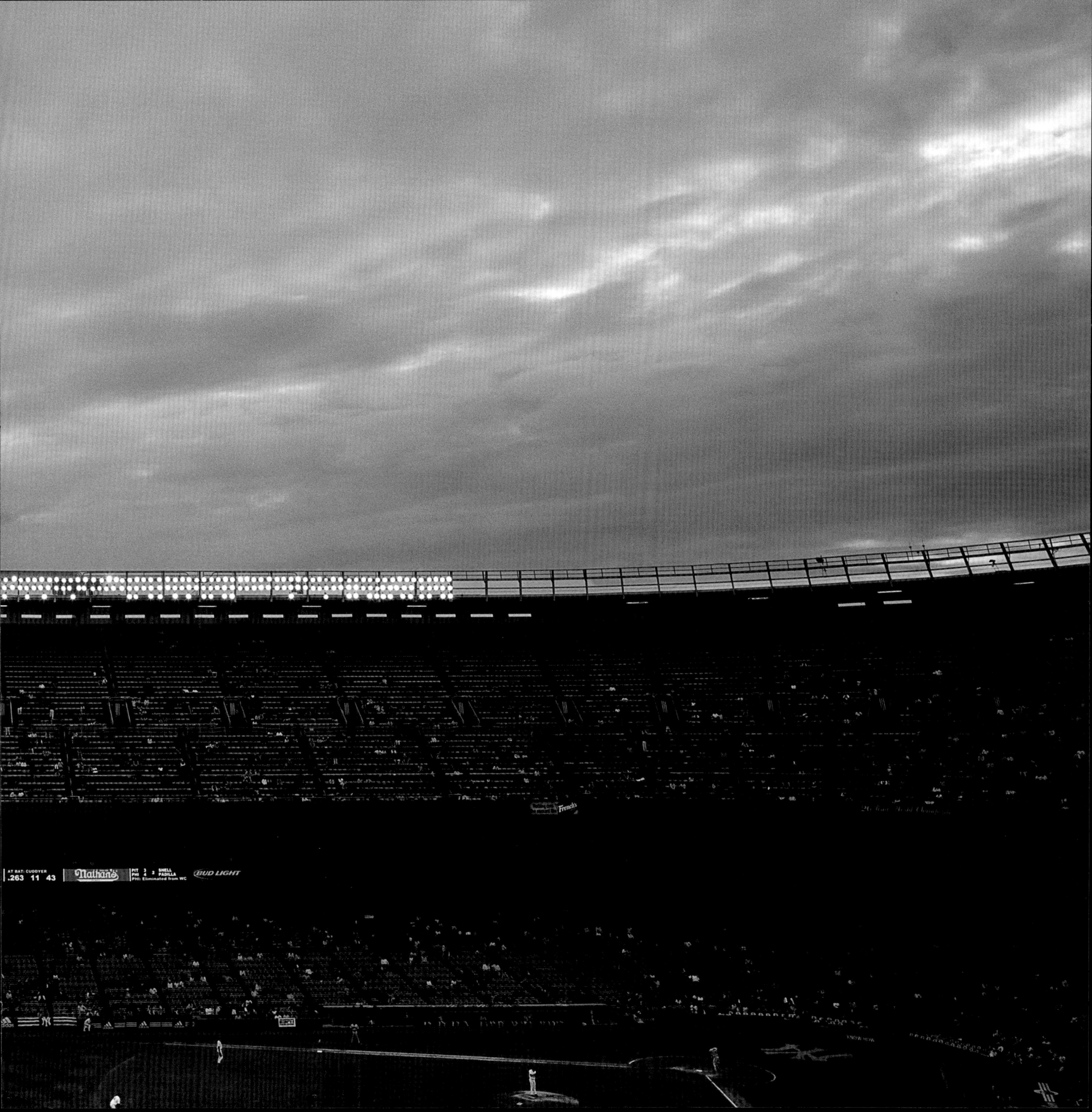
AT BAT: CUDDYER
.263 11 43
Nathan's
PIT 3 SNELL
PHI 4 2 PADILLA
PHI: Eliminated from WC
BUD LIGHT
French's

Going to a Yankee game back in the
teenage friends and I all lived in the

On a Sunday morning, a group of us would be leaning against a building wall and somebody would ask, "Hey, do you want to go to the game?" And we'd all say, "Yeah, let's go." One of the guys would then run up to his apartment and slap together a half-dozen or so salami sandwiches. Then we'd run to the EL—we didn't have much time to spare—and off we'd go.

We usually sat up in the

40s was a spur-of-the-moment thing. My
3ronx.

bleachers for fifty cents.

If we were feeling flush, we'd sit in the stands for a dollar—way up and way back. And we'd sit through both games of a doubleheader.

And the Stadium, it was always so special, it's vastness. I mean, you're not a big guy, and the place was huge. We just hadn't been in that kind of environment before. And the sounds: hearing the bat hit the ball, and the ball going into the glove.

After the game, my friends and I would go onto the field. I'd start to think, boy, if I could ever play here. . . .

I wanted to be a first baseman like my hero Lou Gehrig. So I'd amble up to first base, and picture myself ten years older in a Yankee uniform taking wild throws and making pickups and stretches. Do a little daydreaming—until some cop would yell out, "Okay let's go boys," and then it was back to the subway with thousands of other fans, heading home to my apartment on East 181st Street in the Bronx.

–Al Chasan
A Fan

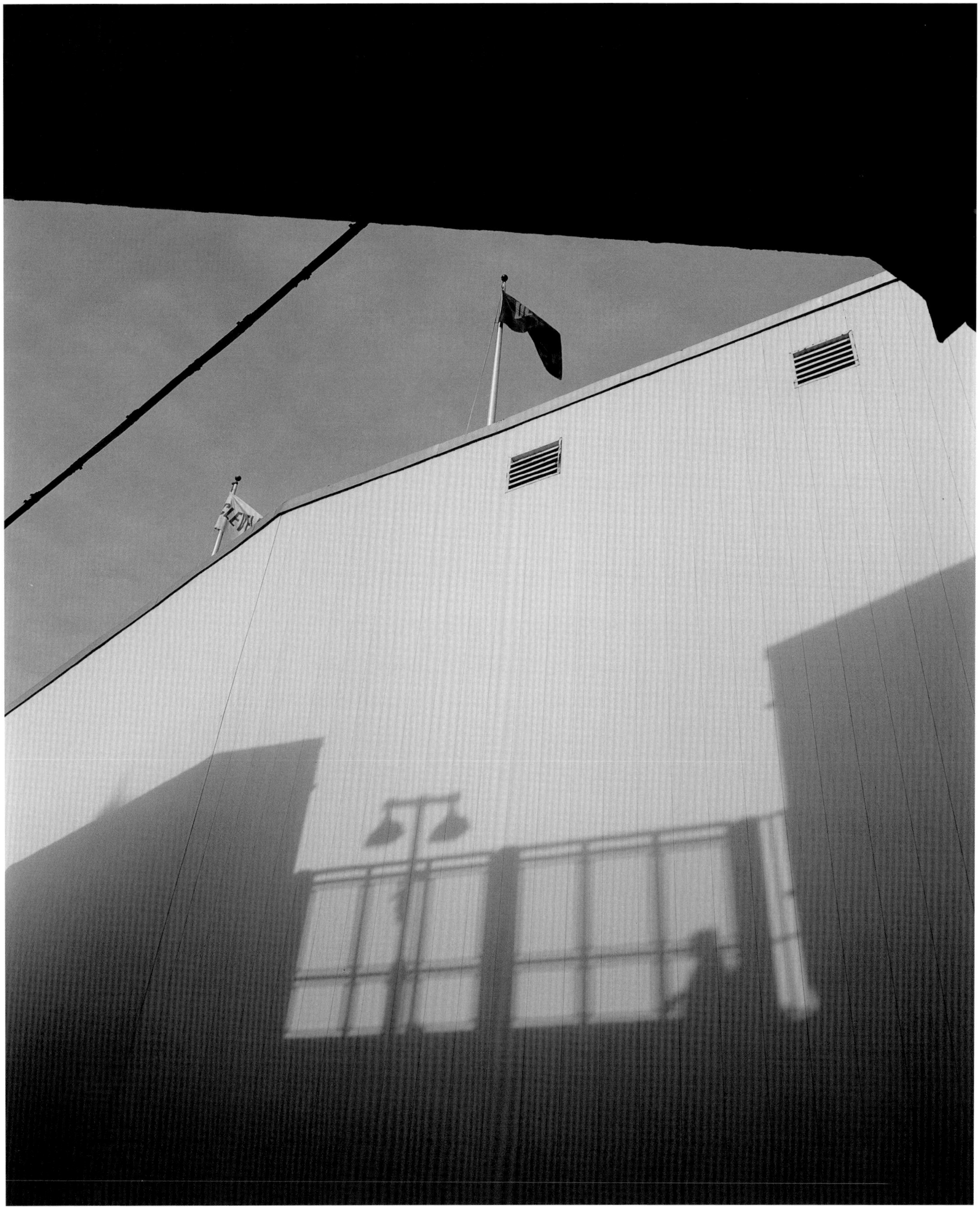

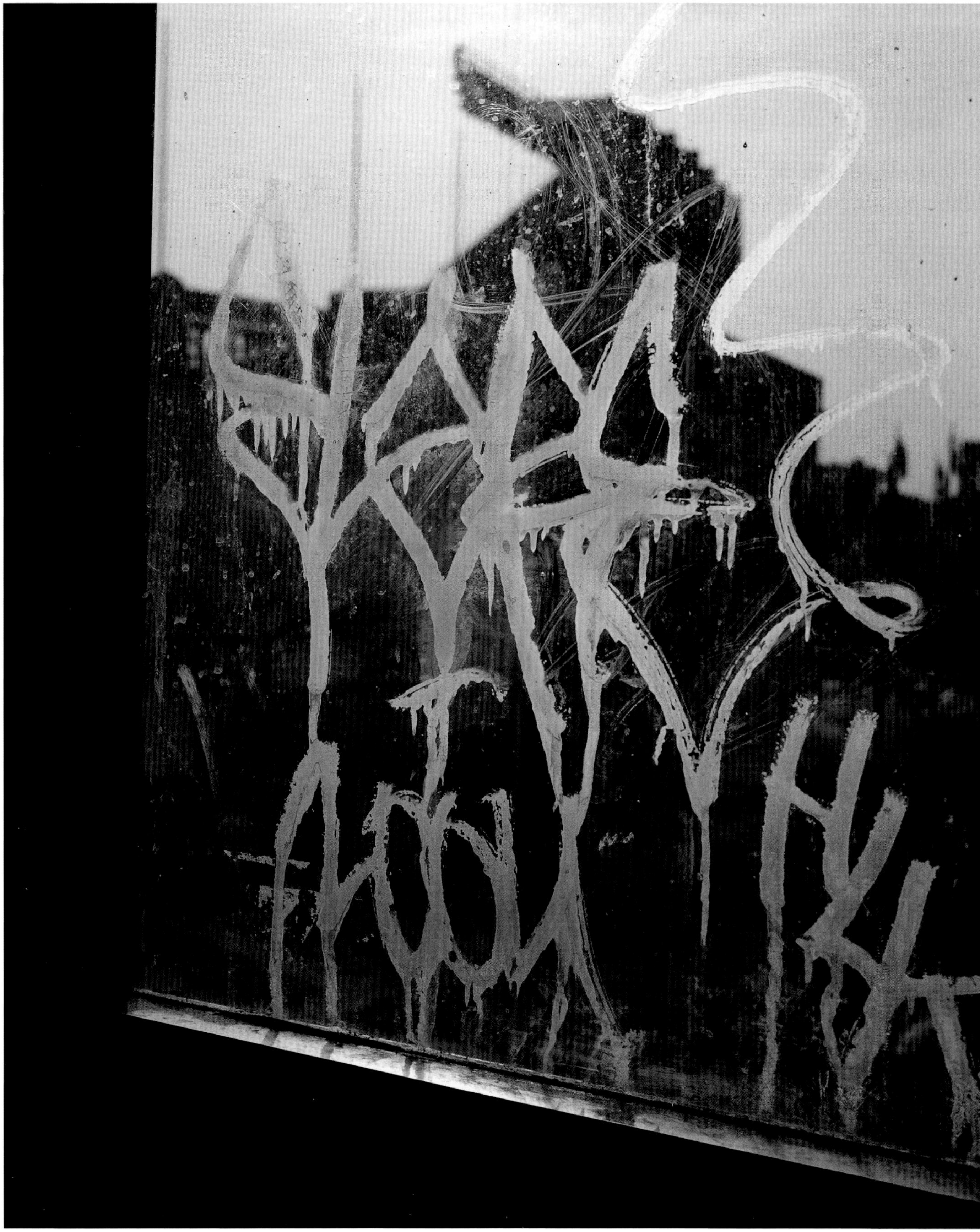

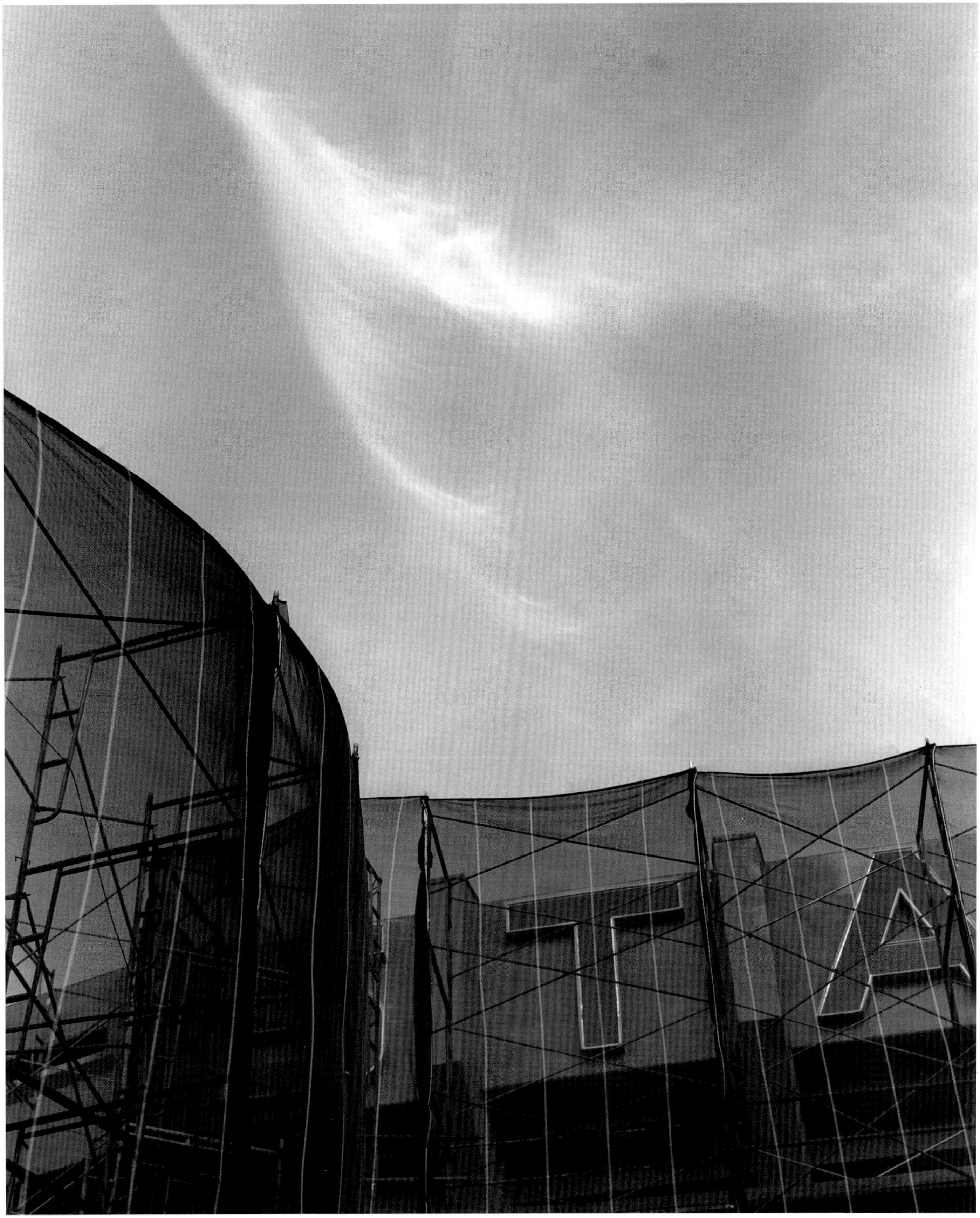

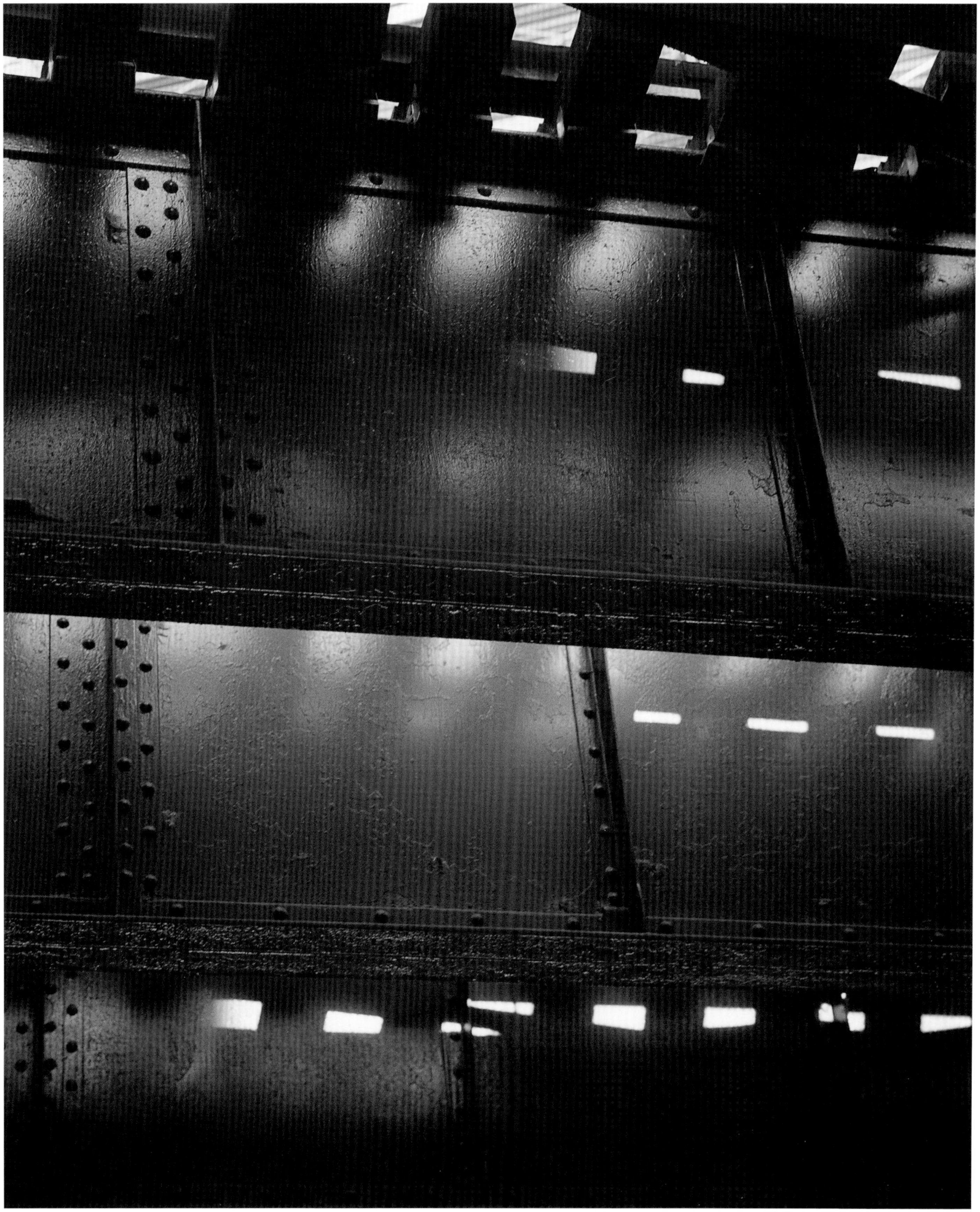

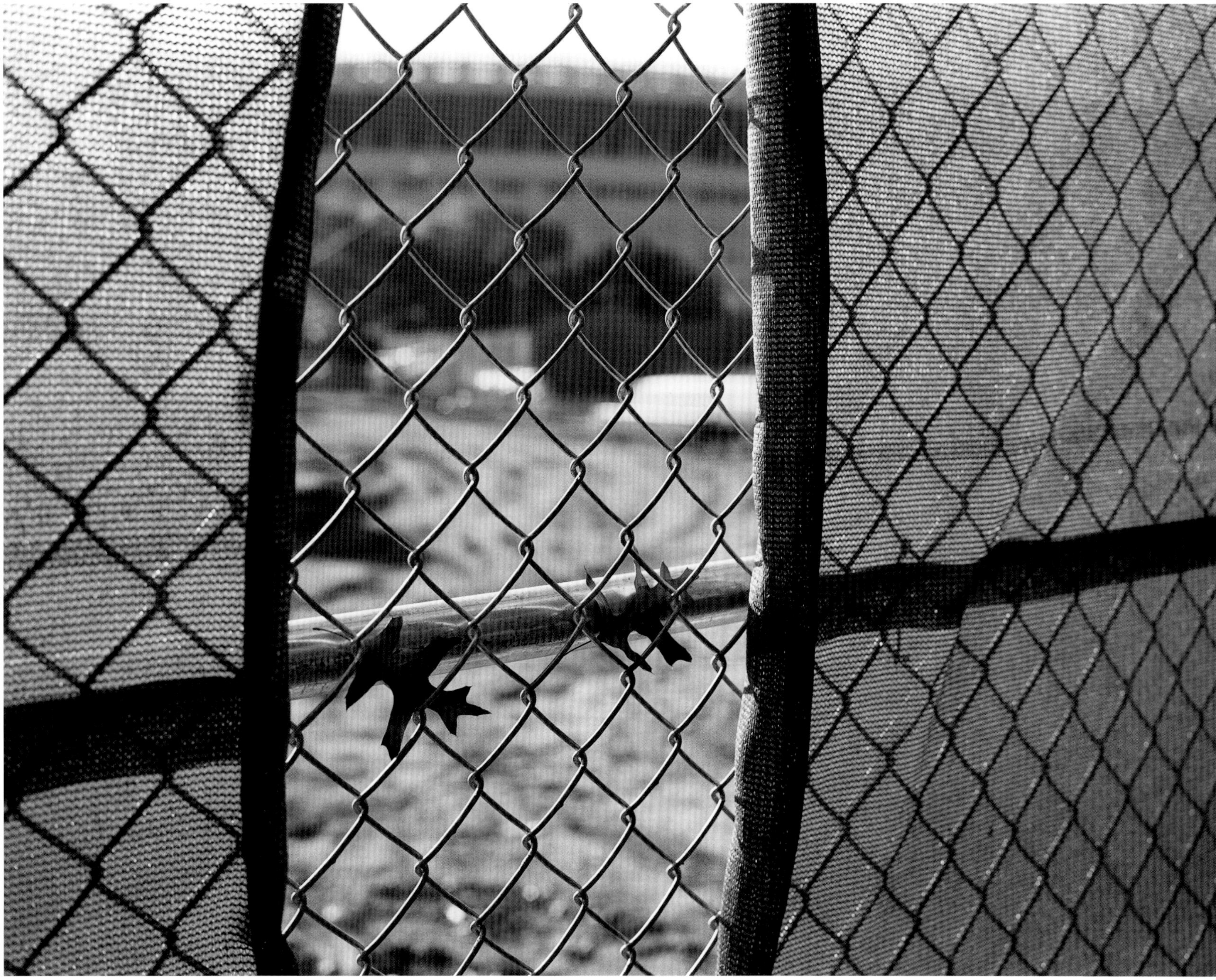

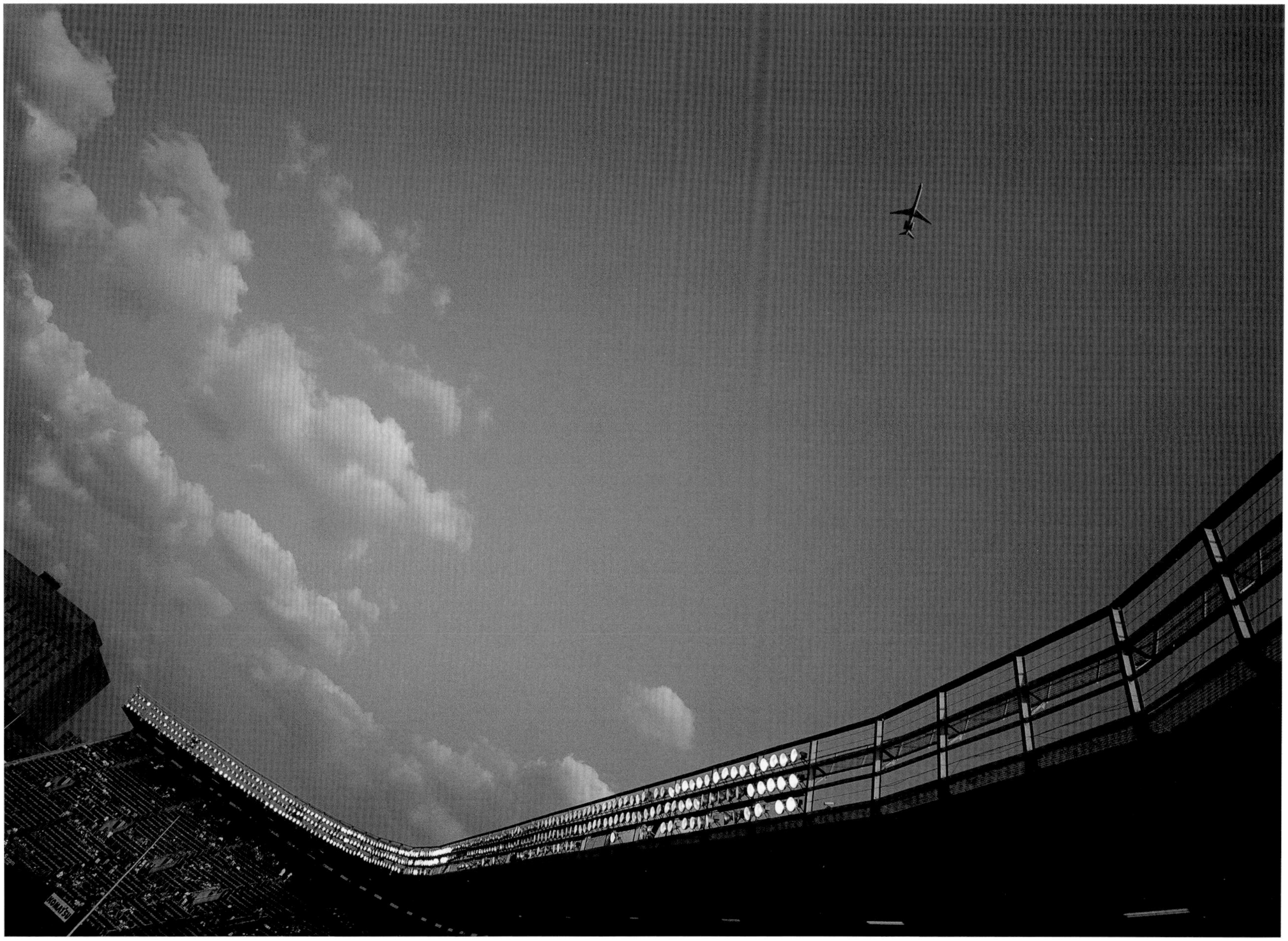

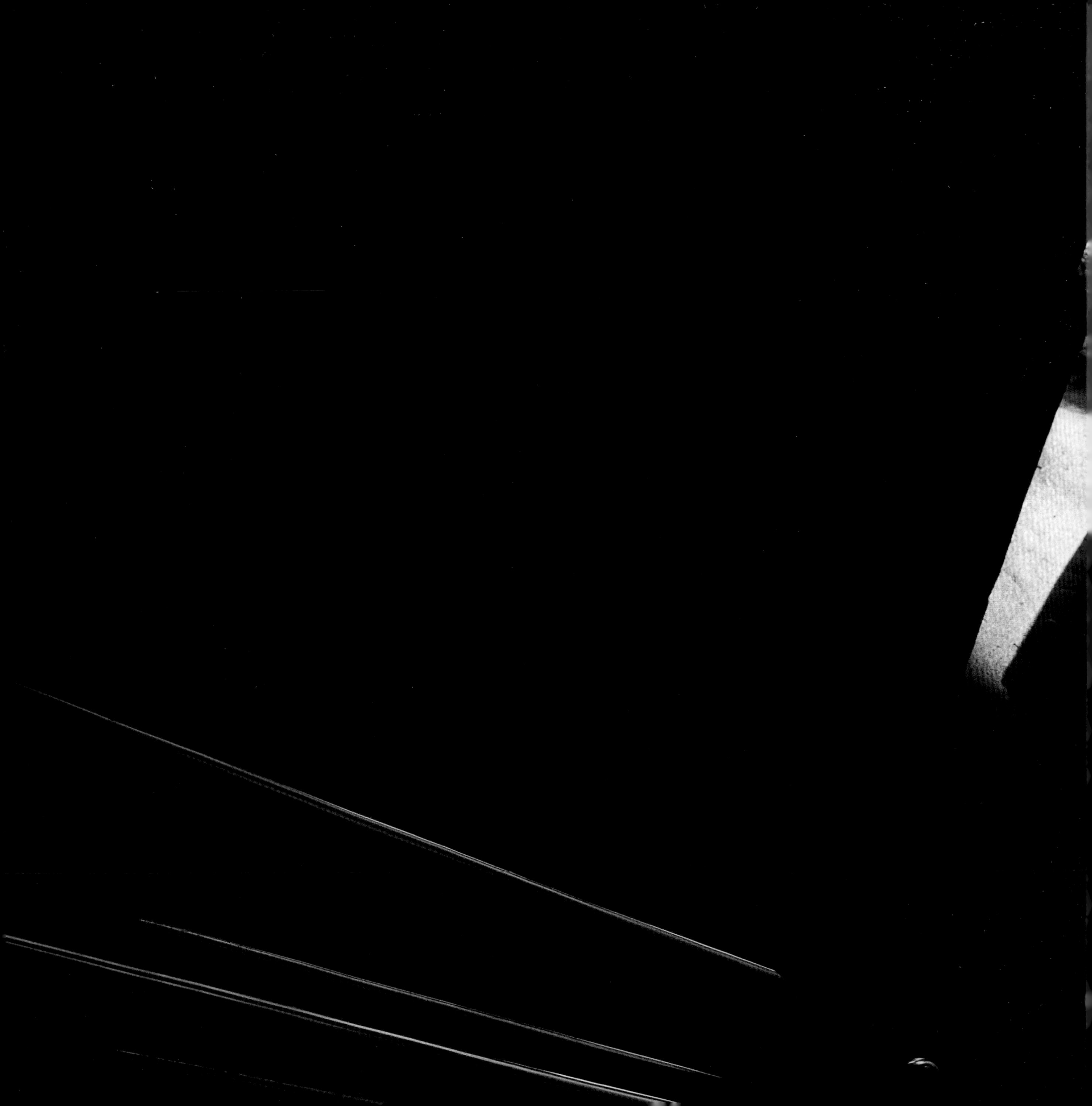

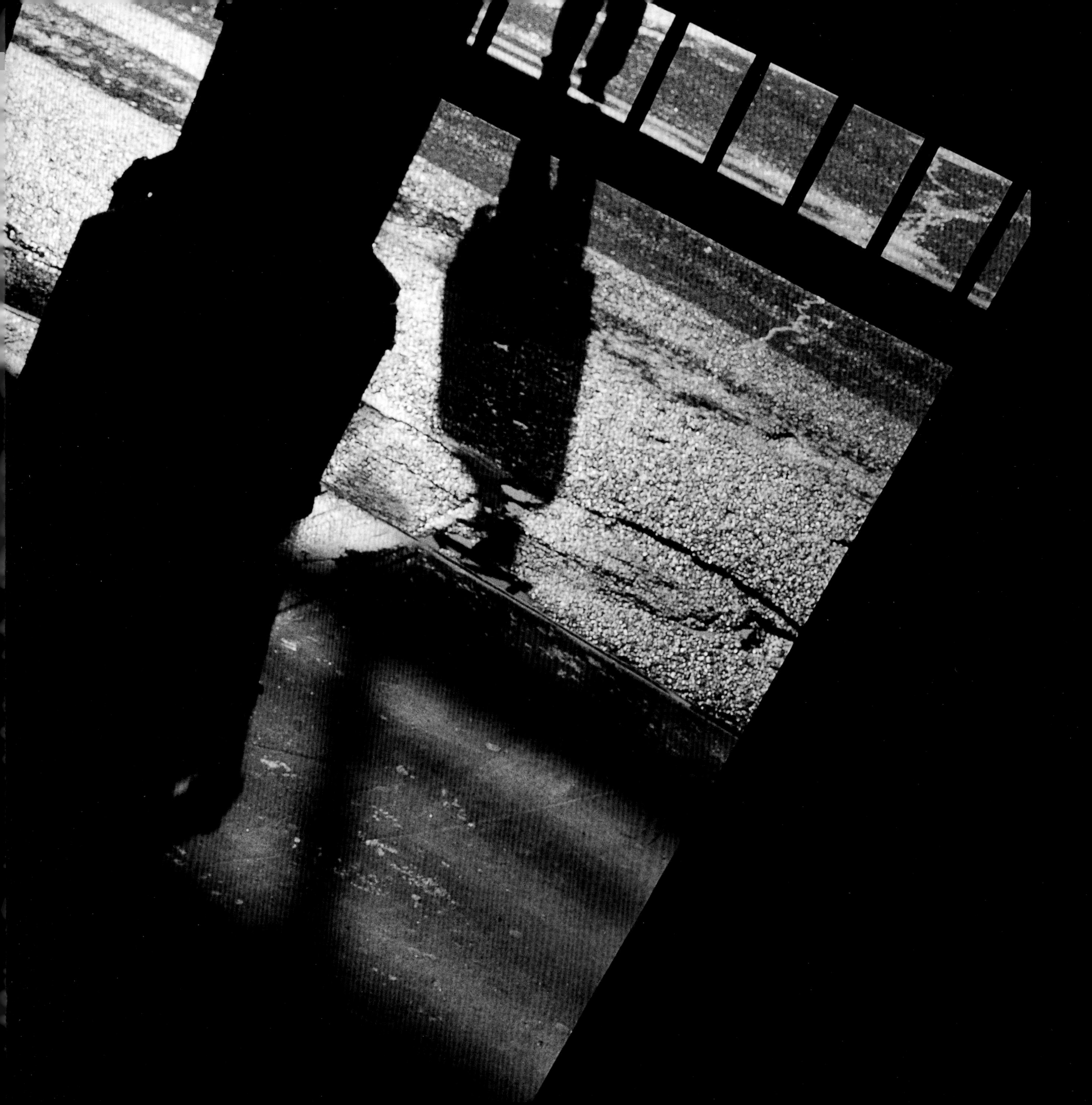

Special thanks to:
David H. Wells, Andy Jacobson, and Chuck Kelton

Published by State University of New York Press, Albany

© 2011 Jon Plasse

All rights reserved

Printed in the United States of America

No part of this book may be used or reproduced in any manner whatsoever without written permission. No part of this book may be stored in a retrieval system or transmitted in any form or by any means including electronic, electrostatic, magnetic tape, mechanical, photocopying, recording, or otherwise without the prior permission in writing of the publisher.

For information, contact State University of New York Press, Albany, NY
www.sunypress.edu

Excelsior Editions is an imprint of State University of New York Press

Production by Ryan Morris
Marketing by Fran Keneston
Design by Andy Jacobson and Stacy Mar
Prints by Kelton Labs, Inc.

Library of Congress Cataloging-in-Publication Data

Plasse, Jon.
The Stadium : Images and Voices of the Original Yankee Stadium / Photographs by Jon Plasse.
p. cm.
ISBN 978-1-4384-4005-7 (hardcover : alk. paper) 1. Yankee Stadium (New York, N.Y. : 1923-2009)—Pictorial works. 2. Yankee Stadium (New York, N.Y. : 1923-2009)—Anecdotes 3. Yankee Stadium (New York, N.Y. : 1923-2009)—History. 4. New York Yankees (Baseball team)—History. I. Title.
GV416.N48P585 2011
796.357068747'1—dc22
2011014226

10 9 8 7 6 5 4 3 2 1